Training Your German Shepherd Dog

Second Edition

Dan Rice, D.V.M.

BARRON'S

About the Author

Writing was an avocation most of Dan Rice's professional life and eventually became his retirement career. Dan is a Colorado veterinarian who obtained a notable understanding of companion dogs as well as competition dogs and their owners through a long personal and professional association with them. His personal knowledge of German Shepherds' intelligence, talents, and idiosyncrasies is coupled with extensive research into training techniques in contemporary use as well as those of the past.

Dan has many other titles to his credit for Barron's, including *Bengal Cats, 2nd ed.; Complete Book of Dog Breeding, 2nd ed.; Complete Book of Cat Breeding; Akitas, 2nd ed.; Dogs from A to Z* (out of print); *The Well-Mannered Cat* (out of print); *Brittanys, 2nd ed.; Chesapeake Bay Retrievers; Spaniels, 2nd ed.; The Dog Handbook; The Beagle Handbook; Big Dog Breeds; West Highland White Terriers; Small Dog Breeds; Bullmastiffs;* and *Pugs*. He also has written several as-yet unpublished novels about animals, including two about Bigfoot.

All inquiries should be addressed to:
Barron's Educational Series, Inc.
250 Wireless Boulevard
Hauppauge, NY 11788
www.barronseduc.com

ISBN-13: 978-0-7641-4320-5
ISBN-10: 0-7641-4320-4

Library of Congress Control No. 2010922743

Printed in China
9 8 7 6 5 4 3 2 1

Acknowledgments

Writing this book was a labor of love, and updating it was a second honeymoon for me. I thank Barron's management, staff, and editors, including Editorial Director Kevin Ryan for allowing me the opportunity to update the 2nd edition of this book and Associate Editor Angela Tartaro for her help. Thanks also goes to Joe Stahlkuppe for the contribution of ideas in his positive evaluation of the 1st edition. Numerous letters received over the past ten years from Shepherd owners and trainers contributed to this 2nd edition by sharing invaluable ideas and information. Special thanks go to Paul and Linda Harms and to Frank and Lacy for their contributions.

A Word About Pronouns

Many dog lovers feel that the pronoun "it" is not appropriate when referring to a pet that can be such a wonderful part of our lives. For this reason, German Shepherds are referred to as "Duchess" or "Duke" throughout this book. These can be applied interchangeably unless the topic specifically relates to a male or female dog.

Cover Credits

Shutterstock: front cover, back cover, inside front cover, inside back cover.

Photo Credits

Norvia Behling: pages 55, 78, 141, 174, 177; Paulette Braun: pages 10, 26, 43, 70, 148; Seth Casteel: pages 16, 19, 39, 45, 49, 64, 67, 85, 168, 181; Kent Dannen: pages 12, 30, 59, 61, 82, 96, 100, 103, 106, 107, 111, 116, 118, 121, 136, 147, 159, 188; Tara Darling: page 150; Cheryl Ertelt: pages 80, 138; Shirley Fernandez: page 62; Jean Fogle: page 99; Isabelle Francais: pages 68, 74, 77, 161; Linda Harms: pages 22, 63, 152, 153; Paulette Johnson: pages 7, 8, 84, 122, 125, 154; Paws on the Run: pages 2, 4, 162; Tom Rice: pages 151, 155, 164, 165, 166; Shutterstock: pages viii, 13, 14, 25, 29, 32, 33, 34, 42, 46, 57, 65, 71, 94, 108, 112, 156, 167, 171, 173, 178, 179; Connie Summers: pages 20, 35, 50, 52, 53, 54, 56, 72, 89, 91, 92, 133; Barbara Young: pages 5, 104.

Contents

1 Introduction

Why Train Your German Shepherd?

Dogs are often obtained by well-meaning people without regard to the magnitude of responsibility inherent in dog ownership. Many puppies of all breeds are obtained without a training plan. The naïveté of certain new dog owners is overwhelming. Their only knowledge of a breed comes from a movie with an outstanding, wonderfully trained canine actor in the hero role. Other equally naïve people become infatuated with dogs they see on television commercials, which depict puppies running to their favorite food, or meticulously groomed, obedient dogs sitting calmly and patiently by their owner's side. Sometimes, a wistful canine glance is thrown in the direction of a sack of the food being promoted. Nothing is said about the hours of grooming, feeding, and training required to produce these actors.

Dog movies are often misleading and not truly representative of the star's breed. These movies may be the cause for overproduction and deterioration of canine stars' breeds. German Shepherds are among the breeds of dogs that have felt the pressure of movie and commercial TV stardom. Unscrupulous breeders produce questionable-quality puppies to satisfy a temporary market. Consumers, fascinated with a particular dog, buy any puppy resembling the star.

A family obtains a dog then leaves it to its own devices. Without thought to the harm being caused by its lack of training, it is neglected in the backyard for months at a time. The pup is fed, watered, and sometimes invited to play, but mostly it gradually grows into a magnificent nuisance and the owner then becomes angry with the dog because it has no manners. The dog won't come when it's called; it escapes from the yard at every opportunity and stays away all day. Neighbors complain about the barking. It chews the fingers off baseball gloves, tears stockings, muddies clothes, punctures the garden hose, and the last straw is when the owner's expensive new running shoe is reduced to shredded rubber.

The owner is heard to complain: "After the price I paid for him and more money spent on vaccinations and dog food! How dare that mutt ruin my $200 shoe?"

This owner has a huge chip on his shoulder, and he makes up his mind to

"teach this dog some manners, once and for all!" He proceeds on a collision course with the dog, which is willing to be taught, but reluctant to be bullied. Needless to say, with such an attitude, the dog learns nothing, the owner is furious and indignant, and the dog winds up in the pound.

Training is a fundamental part of owning and maintaining any pet, especially a German Shepherd Dog. Shepherds are sensitive, smart, and easily trained dogs, but we humans have not yet bred a dog with auto-programming. A well-trained dog will bring joy to its owner all its life, but an untrained dog—ignored, bored, and lonely—is a sad, wasted creature. Many become liabilities to their families and the community in which they live.

If you are contemplating the purchase of a German Shepherd puppy or you have already obtained such a pup and find yourself learning instead of teaching, you need help. If the pup has taken over the household and is chewing everything in sight, jumping up on you and tearing your clothes, or frightening the children, it's time to turn the situation around. It's easy and fun to own a well-trained German Shepherd Dog, and you'll be amazed when you see how much love and satisfaction it will provide you and your family if it is given the opportunity. If you want to start out on the right foot in your training program, read on.

You can't start training too early, but, owing to the Shepherd's intelligence and trainability, you can begin at any time of life. It is never too late to begin or too early to start!

Canine Origin and Domestication

In order to show a dog how to learn, we must know something of its history, inherited characteristics, and instincts. According to contemporary scientists who have discovered by application of mitochondrial (intracellular) DNA analysis, the wolf and dog had a common ancestor, or all dogs are descended from wolves. Lest you get the wrong impression, it is probable that different types of wolves were tamed and eventually domesticated in dozens if not hundreds of different prehistoric human cultures and communities. Thus, the genetic composition of different dogs may vary slightly because they "originated" in different parts of the world from different races of wolves.

Similarities Between Dogs and Wolves

The similarities of dogs and wolves are significant, including their pack mentality, which facilitates specialized training. Whether or not we concede that wolves were really the progenitors of dogs, the species have many features in common:

- Both have teeth adapted to seizing, slicing, and tearing, rather than chewing.
- Both have extremely acute senses of smell and hearing.
- Domestic dogs, like their wolf forefathers, follow the guidance of the alpha dog, or dominant member of their pack. Feral dogs, like wolves, maintain

central headquarters, regions, or dens, which they defend.

Knowing these facts gives us a tremendous advantage when we set a course of training for our Shepherd.

Differentiating Features of Wolves and Dogs

Scholars have sometimes differentiated dogs from wolves by the dog's propensity to bark, and the wolf's inability, or lack of desire, to do so. However, it has been proven that tamed wolves can learn to bark when the reason for barking is important to assure survival. By the same token, many wild dogs, and a few domestic ones, do not bark.

Many other features of domestic dogs separate them from their wolf ancestors both in appearance and personality.

- Dogs in general have a shorter muzzle and rounder eyes than do wolves. This is probably due to neoteny, the word used to describe juvenile features that appear in an adult. These juvenile characteristics were no doubt selectively bred into wolves as they were being tamed to give them a more domesticated appearance.
- Other juvenile characteristics seen in dogs are smiles or other facial expressions, and behavioral habits such as the tendency to frolic and play even in old age.
- Another feature of wolves, which has been eliminated from most dogs, is neophobia, or a fear of new things. Selective breeding was probably employed to reduce neophobia; the results were more stable personalities and less shyness and timidity in dogs.

Thinking, Planning, and Reasoning

Dogs use sophisticated reasoning powers to solve problems. Wolves and other feral Canidae (canine family) often hold part of their hunting pack in reserve to wait until their prey has been fatigued by the chase. When the victim tires, a few fresh, rested dogs jump into the fray, rush the quarry, and make the kill. In these wolf packs, the youngest and most agile run the prey, and the strongest, most experienced hunters are held in reserve to make the kill.

Wild Canidae can probably sense wounded quarry, and realize that these animals present easier targets. Bird dogs use their memories and reasoning ability to solve retrieving problems. They deduce that wounded birds must be retrieved before those that were killed by the hunter's gun, and they circle or quarter in the hunting field to find the scent of an injured bird.

Dogs have been known to prove their instinctive loyalty to humans by pulling a drowning child from a swimming pool, warning sleeping owners of a fire, or leading sightless masters around a pot-hole in their path. None of these actions is specifically taught to the dog, yet the canine mind somehow reasons and thinks out the problem, then plans and initiates an appropriate action.

Graphic examples are reported almost daily illustrating a dog's reasoning powers and devotion to its family, in which it acts not according to survival instincts, but by thinking.

Human Influence

Ancient canines lived in family packs, which were no doubt much like prehistoric human communities. These wolves or wild dogs probably vied with humans for an equal place in the food chain. Cave dwellers and wolves had many of the same predators and prey. Like their human counterparts, wolves shared a desire for warm, easily defendable dens, and existed on a diet similar to human fare. It seems these two species were destined to become companions and hunting partners, joining their intelligence and adaptability to serve each other.

Humans and canines have established a mutually beneficial relationship predating written history. Petroglyphs decorating walls of prehistoric human cave homes depict the symbiotic association the two species enjoyed. This kinship is confirmed by the paintings and sculptures of dogs found among relics of ancient civilizations.

Domestication

Canines were undoubtedly the first animal species to be domesticated by humans. Wolflike carnivores survived by hunting, killing, and eating their prey, or by scavenging from the prey killed by other carnivores. In the earliest human-wolf relationships, wolves may have trained themselves to follow cave-dwelling humans on hunts to forage from the leftovers of the quarry primitive men managed to slaughter. It's equally possible the opposite is true and cavemen learned to follow a hunting pack and scavenge from wolves' kill.

Prehistoric humans were predators with larger brains than those of wolves. These people probably had rudimentary abstract reasoning capability, advanced communication capacity, and the all-important opposable thumb. The wolf, for its part, had many important intrinsic qualities as well. The human hunter probably recognized the value of the four-legged animal's speed, strength, and endurance, and rather than compete, they joined forces.

To survive with man, a dog had to recognize the human as the dominant or alpha member of its pack. Domestication was probably begun when wolf puppies were taken from their dens at a very early age, raised, trained, and selectively bred by humans. These wolf pups may have been handled, fed, and carried about by cave children. By the time they were grown, they expressed a certain degree of trust and bonding with humans. The more manageable or trainable wolves formed the gene pool that was used to propagate the species. Eventually, the domestic dog was created.

Wolves' innate abilities such as their endurance and highly developed olfactory system, or sense of smell, made them worthwhile partners. Early dog breeders must have recognized the dogs' scenting and trailing aptitude and made use of those gifts.

Division of labor within a human community might have given certain humans the responsibility of caring for the dogs; thus were born prehistoric dog trainers and handlers. Later, with canine help, certain herbivorous animals could be captured, herded, protected, and killed for food, clothing, and tools.

Dogs sharing human dwellings and food supplies would naturally guard these possessions from predators, whether those predators were wolves or strange humans. Eventually, various sizes and types of dogs were purposefully bred to serve a particular need of the human, such as coursing, killing, guarding, or herding.

If a dog refused to submit to human domination, it was eliminated. If it couldn't live up to its job description, the dog was rejected from human society and became meat for stew pots and pelts for clothing. By this primitive but practical selective breeding, only the most useful dogs were kept to become helpmates to the people who fed, housed, and bred them.

Ancient Times

Dogs of ancient times were recognized as valuable members of society. In the seventh century A.D. a folk law assessed heavy fines for anyone who killed a herdsman's dog.

In 1494 Petrus de Crescentis, a Greek instructor of agriculture, documented many lasting tenets in his book, *Field and Furrow Cultivation*. He wrote: ". . . shepherds shall take right good care of their dogs . . . . Our daily needs lays it upon us

that we must first have good [dog] track-ers that they may hunt up the wolves and track them."

He goes on to say: "The manor house and property should be guarded by large and mighty dogs that are a terror to thieves and other knaves." He further states: "Owners should make their dogs comfort-able nests, and they must train them with patience." Thus, even in the fifteenth cen-tury, dog training was emphasized and the operative word was "patience."

Selective Breeding

It was only natural for dominant humans to select, propagate, and train only the type(s) of dogs that pleased them, the dogs that could and would do what needed to be done. Thus, by continued selective breeding, we now have hun-dreds of different breeds, incorporating various sizes, abilities, and temperaments from which to choose.

The German Shepherd has risen to the top of the list of these utilitarian creatures as a valuable and loyal accom-plice in virtually every human endeavor.

Breeding Methods
The Canis species' genetic makeup is highly malleable. Techniques similar to those used in the past are currently being used by modern dog breeders to modify or accentuate physical and men-tal characteristics, such as size, color, trainability, intelligence, and tempera-ment. However, selective breeding is not perfect and often goes awry.

2 History of the German Shepherd Dog

German Shepherd Dog Origin

Individual skills form the basis for many of the jobs we train our dogs to do. When one considers the many capabilities of *Canis familiaris* (the domestic dog), we can get an idea of why certain dogs evolved into their present-day sizes and shapes. To understand how and why German Shepherd Dogs came to be, we must look at the available literature.

An early German Shepherd breeder and writer, Max Emil Friedrich von Stephanitz, a German cavalry captain, wrote in his 1925 book that the German Shepherd descended from a Bronze Age progenitor. He identified this Shepherd ancestor as *Canis poutiatini*, a Neolithic dog found near Moscow. He identified another ancestor, the Hovawart, a German domestic guard dog dating from the thirteenth century and used to protect both livestock and property.

Von Stephanitz also traced the German Shepherd Dog to the writings of the early Roman era by quoting Tacitus, a Roman historian. Tacitus briefly mentioned "a wolflike dog," seen in the Rhine country of Germany. This led von Stephanitz to imply that the dog mentioned was a progenitor of the German Shepherd.

According to von Stephanitz, the Bronze Age Shepherd dog accompanied its masters as they progressed from nomadic hunters to cattle tenders, then to their farms where they began to till the soil and breed livestock. As this human development moved forward from hunters to agrarians, the ancestors of today's German Shepherds accompanied them as guard dogs and herd dogs.

Acquired Traits

According to von Stephanitz, German Shepherd Dogs have acquired certain traits through experience. Their instinctive characteristics have broadened to include the result of work in service extending over "thousands" of years, toiling alongside human partners, helping manage flocks and herds.

From this extensive experience with livestock, the hereditary attributes of the Shepherd formed, and eventually the dog became suitable for every other conceivable type of work as well. However, training is still needed to augment or fortify the breed's natural, instinctive endowments and to produce predictable results in the many other vocations in which this breed excels.

Captain von Stephanitz, a learned writer and researcher, also commented on the personality of German Shepherds. He suggests the typical German Shepherd will tolerate strict discipline, but is too independent to be constantly ordered about. Shepherds must be carefully and gently taught, not drilled, into each new endeavor.

Max von Stephanitz's book, *The German Shepherd Dog in Word and Picture*, contains a very colorful and academic history of all dogs, with concentration on the Shepherd. The book is filled with theories, pictures, charts, diagrams, and hypotheses relative to the domestication and training of early dogs. It is available on loan from the U.S.D.A. National Library, NAL Building, 10301 Baltimore Boulevard, Beltsville, Maryland 20705-2351, or can be purchased from the Hoflin Publishing Company, 4401 Zephyr Street, Wheat Ridge, Colorado 80033-3299.

Other Breeds in the German Shepherd's Background

The German Shepherd Dog as we know it probably originated in the middle to late nineteenth century when European farmers developed dogs to tend their herds of cattle and sheep. Sheepdogs were undoubtedly first farm dogs without formal records of their parentage. Pedigree and ancestry were immaterial providing the dogs performed the jobs they were asked to do. In short, these Shepherds were dogs bred to work, and were given the responsibility of guarding flocks of sheep, protecting herds of cattle, and keeping their charges gathered together.

The early sheepdog was probably a herding type rather than a breed. Its conformation, size, coat type, and color weren't necessarily uniform with, or even similar to, other dogs of the same type. However, its instinctive intelligence, trainability, strength, and guarding traits were quite similar. These "tending and warding-off" dogs evolved into the German Shepherd Dog of today.

Characteristics of Shepherds

Early Shepherds were large dogs, tough enough to fend off predator attacks on livestock. They had sufficient intelligence

An All-Around Dog

The German Shepherd is in the herding group. However, it might have been placed into another AKC group because of its talent, intelligence, and common uses. That group is the working group, which includes breeds like the Akita, Rottweiler, Boxer, and Standard Schnauzer. All of these breeds are similar in size and may be trained in similar uses. The versatile Shepherd is often Schutzhund trained for police work, has performed for years guiding the blind, and is easily trained to be a superior guard dog. The Shepherd also has great scenting abilities that sometimes match hounds' tracking prowess. The German Shepherd is commonly used in drug-sniffing endeavors and in search-and-rescue duties.

The dog would not only protect their flock, it could take them to and from pasture, corral them, and act as a shepherd in practically every management function.

The gene pool of this breed may have been mixed with those of other similar European breeds belonging to the Dutch, Belgians, and French, but by the late 1800s the German Shepherd Dog was recognized as a distinct and separate breed.

It is likely that von Stephanitz chose his own breeding stock from those working shepherds of the nineteenth century. He was apparently well versed in animal husbandry and selective breeding. This scholar undoubtedly had great influence on the early development and standardization of this wonderful breed, and is often referred to as the "Father of the German Shepherd."

Development of the German Shepherd Dog

During World War I, German Shepherd Dogs were commonly trained as draft animals in Europe, usually harnessed in pairs or sometimes in threes. They were occasionally harnessed under light horse carts or pony carts to add dogpower to horsepower.

Perhaps as early as 1882, but certainly by 1891, the Phylax Society came into being and sponsored the breed, but this group of enthusiasts faded. (Phylax is a Greek word meaning a watchman or guard.) The argument that apparently caused the downfall of the Phylax Society was similar to one heard today:

and cleverness to outwit other large carnivores and were taught to track wolves and other predators and destroy them.

These dogs were quite valuable with another instinctive and indispensable characteristic; Shepherds have a possessive personality. Through long experience, they inherently recognize a responsibility to their masters and their livestock. This personality feature, a sense of proprietorship, has been passed down for generations in the German Shepherd. Von Stephanitz wrote that the "sheepdog" became the "Shepherd" when its owners and breeders recognized that the dog could actually replace a human shepherd.

1. One faction of German Shepherd fanciers wanted the breed to be recognized as working herd dogs with sufficient reasoning ability and power to herd, guard, and protect their charges. They felt a dog show was nothing more than a beauty contest.
2. The opposing group of fanciers wanted to fix the Shepherd type as a show dog, with the primary emphasis on beauty rather than functional ability.

Conscientious German Shepherd breeders of today are doing their best to combine these two views to produce a sound utility dog with style and beauty as well.

Herding Ability

The history of the German Shepherd as a highly trainable herding breed continued in 1896 when the gene pool included herding dogs of the Wurtemberg type, the Thuringian type, and the Swabian type. The Wurtemberg dogs contributed the tail carriage and variety of color markings typical of today's Shepherd, the

Thuringian gave the breed erect ears and prominent wolf gray color, and the Swabian working dog genes were added for stamina, courage, strength, and speed.

The variety of herding breeds used to develop the German Shepherd produced a diversity of appearances in the breed for a few years, until it became somewhat standardized through selective breeding. In 1895 the breed was still found in three coat types, smooth, long-haired, and wire-haired. Today, only the smooth and long-haired varieties are seen.

Police Work

These intelligent and talented dogs were in great demand as guarding and herding dogs until fences, railroads, and other means of collecting and moving flocks evolved. At the same time, other methods of predator control usurped the dog's guarding duties. By then, fanciers of the breed recognized the value of their dogs, and instead of allowing this fine utility breed to die out, they used the dogs' intelligence and trainability to move them into other roles, primarily associated with police and guard work. The breed was an immediate success in police departments all across their country of origin as well as in other nations.

War Dogs

German Shepherd Dogs found yet another niche in war service during World War I in Germany, as well as in France, Belgium, Austria, England, and later, the United States. Once again, lessons were never too difficult for these dogs to comprehend and their instructors were never too exacting for the intelligent Shepherd. They were able to understand the reason for each new task they were given.

National Loyalty

The years of international conflict saw the popularity of German Shepherds wane in the allied Western countries. This reduced production of Shepherds was due entirely to its name. Of course, "German" Shepherd Dogs had no politics; they recognized no national allegiance. They were loyal to their masters, regardless of their country of origin or the language in which they received their commands.

The British, not wishing to forgo this dog's usefulness, struggled with the dog's name, and finally changed it to "Alsatian." This seemed to eliminate the stigma attached to the use of "German" dogs during Hitler's reign of terror. Later, the term "Wolf Dog" was added to their name, and the Alsatian Wolf Dog Club was formed in 1919 in England.

The name Alsatian Wolf Dog is actually a misnomer. It is unlikely that the breed contains any wolf blood, at least none acquired in recent history. The wolf is a predator, and in order to produce a wolf-dog cross that would instinctively protect sheep and perform the many other duties set for them by mankind, the wolf's predatory hunt-and-kill instinct would need to be suppressed. It seems very doubtful that such a feat could be accomplished in a few generations. No one would take a streamlined, biddable, intelligent dog such as the German Shepherd

and cross it with a wild animal with typical wolf conformation and personality.

The German Shepherd Dog Club of America was founded in 1912 in the United States. During the rise of the Third Reich, the word "German" stuck in the throat of many American dog fanciers, who sometimes responded by dropping the country of origin from the dog's name. The dogs thus were commonly called Shepherds in the United States during and after World War I. Some people preferred to call the animals police dogs. Regardless of what it was called, the breed stayed the same and was recognized as one of the most intelligent and trainable dogs in the world.

Trainability Leads to Stardom

Strongheart. Following World War I, a German Shepherd Dog named Etzel was brought to the United States by Bruno Hoffman. This dog soon became the property of Jane Murfin, who subsequently teamed up with Larry Trimble, a dog trainer. Etzel went to Hollywood and quickly captured the American eye as the accomplished canine movie star "Strongheart."

"German Shepherd" soon became synonymous with "Strongheart" in the imagination of the American movie-going public. Lawrence Armour of Chicago imported Etzel's sire, Nores von der Kriminalpoletzi, and virtually every available Shepherd female was bred to this dog.

Rin Tin Tin. Another dog of superior intelligence rose to even greater heights in the American movies; he came from Europe a few years later. Rin Tin Tin, or Rinty, was born in 1916 in a German trench at Metz, where he was abandoned by the German soldiers as they retreated. He was found in a German dugout and nursed through puppyhood by American Army Lieutenant Lee Duncan, who in civilian life was a trainer of police dogs in Santa Monica, California. Rinty was first trained in police work, but when his great aptitude and trainability were discovered, he was taken to Los Angeles. There he earned a contract with Warner Brothers where he starred in many silent films. Rinty died in 1932, but his son acted in his role for a few years, and afterward, several other German Shepherds played Rinty in the television series bearing his name.

Thousands of purported relatives of Strongheart and Rinty,

including "cousins" and "sisters" of these dogs and their offspring, flooded the American market. Infatuated, gullible Americans flocked to buy them. Everyone wanted a son or daughter, brother or sister of Strongheart or Rinty. If every German Shepherd sold as a "son of Rinty" was actually Rinty's pup, Rin Tin Tin would have gone down in the Guinness Book of World Records as the most prolific dog of all times.

German Shepherd breeders flourished; they sold thousands of pitiful specimens of the breed, many with phony pedigrees and no registration. Why was the American public so easily duped? These two German Shepherd canine movie stars were exceptionally smart and remarkably trainable. Their trainers used the dogs' intelligence to develop skills so amazing they caught and held public acclaim.

Overbreeding

As is often the case, overproduction brought about a deterioration of the breed. Dogs resembling a German Shepherd were bred to alleged cousins, sisters, or brothers of Rin Tin Tin or Strongheart. Eventually this overproduction cooled down, but not before it took its toll. The extreme popularity of German Shepherds in the United States, coupled with the importation of culls and misfits from German breeding programs, infused many undesirable characteristics into the breed in America. Shyness, timidity, aggressiveness, poor conformation, and other problems plagued American Shepherds. Newspapers were filled with articles telling of attacking and biting incidents by "German police dogs."

American Adoption

During the years prior to World War II, well-bred German Shepherds continued to make a name for themselves in the United States. Due to the breed's mentality and proficiency, the Shepherd was selected as the official dog of both the U.S. Navy and the U.S. Coast Guard. Its coat was regarded as the best for all types of weather; it thrived in every terrain, allowing trained dogs to be sent to any area of need.

At about the same time, the highly trainable Shepherd became famous for leading our sightless population, and contributed greatly to the blending of those people into everyday society.

For two consecutive years between World War I and World War II, the German Shepherd Dog accounted for one third of all American Kennel Club (AKC) registrations. It proved to be an affectionate, easily trained family pet, a guard dog for industry, and a talented police dog. Those duties hardly scratch the surface of its skills. While this dog's personality and physical conformation suffered a great deal from mass production and inbreeding, the intelligence and aptitude of the German Shepherd were compromised very little. The Shepherd continued to prove itself as the best of the utility breeds.

During and after World War II, many American soldiers returned home accompanied by more of their newfound friends, and German Shepherd Dogs were trained and became proficient as hearing dogs, handicap aids, lifeguards, and scent dogs that sometimes challenged the Bloodhound's skill. These many gifts were found in a breed originally used to tend and guard flocks, one developed specifically to outclass the Scottish Collie in strength of jaw and speed.

Admirable Traits

The German Shepherd Dog loves training, especially if the style of the tutor includes plenty of praise and attention. A dog easily raised with children, the Shepherd will play games with them by the hour. A clean dog with a gentle disposition, it is a class act in every way. Though the Shepherd began over a century ago as a farm dog, a crossbred used to protect flocks from robbers and wolves, it has evolved into a natural family dog.

Shepherds have sufficient brain power to amuse themselves, but they prefer human interaction. Bad temper is occasionally a problem, but no more so than in other breeds. When a shy, nervous, or aggressive German Shepherd is found, the results are often more serious because of the dog's size and strength. For this reason alone, a judicious selection process is demanded when shopping for a companion of this breed.

The sterling character of today's German Shepherd Dog is combined with its remarkable ability to learn. Our challenge is to teach it, train it, and direct this great capability toward useful goals.

3 *Selection*

Are You Ready for a Dog?

Before deciding to acquire a Shepherd to train, there are a few questions you should ask yourself regarding a new dog in the family. Buying a pet on impulse usually leads to disappointment, often of disastrous proportions. Owning a dog for any reason requires a long-term commitment deserving careful thought by its owners. This puppy will share your home and heart for many years and the decision to obtain it should be discussed with, and clearly understood by, all household members.

Timing

In order to get a pup started correctly, everyone in the family must be ready for it. Don't buy your puppy immediately before the holiday season, lest it become lost among new toys. It would be better to purchase dog equipment and a picture of the pup to place under the Christmas tree. Bring the puppy home after the holiday is past and the family has settled into its normal routine.

Do you usually take a vacation in the summer? If you plan to be gone the first few weeks of July, don't bring your new pup home during May or June. In order to train a pup, you must be at home; you can't delegate this responsibility to a friend or boarding kennel. Consistency is the key to housebreaking and leash training, and it is better not to interrupt training while you take a vacation.

Schoolchildren usually change their routine during spring break. Keep this in mind and don't bring a new puppy into an atmosphere of confusion.

A Veterinarian's Opinion

When choosing a new Shepherd pup, consult with knowledgeable people. Talk with a veterinarian about your choice of breed and your training plans. In all probability, he or she has had experience with German Shepherds and will be able to provide insights on your selection. A veterinarian's opinion is invaluable; she or he handles many breeds of dogs every day, and has first-hand experience with the idiosyncrasies and qualities of those breeds.

A prepurchase discussion with your veterinarian serves many purposes:

1. You can gain a general idea of the expense involved in routine dog health care, and boarding kennels available in the area can be discussed.

2. Risks of certain diseases indigenous to your region of the country can be discussed.
3. Prevalent hereditary diseases of Shepherds can be outlined and you may receive advice on how to deal with these and other commonly recognized problems.
4. A veterinarian may even be able to recommend reliable German Shepherd breeders, owners, and trainers in your locality.

Points to Consider

Male or Female?

In the Shepherd, both sexes are strong, loyal, trainable, affectionate, and playful. There is very little gender difference when looking for a pet or companion that will be neutered at or before adulthood. If a female is chosen, the cost of spaying might be a bit more than the cost of castration of a male, but when prorated over the life of the dog, cost is a minor consideration. Either sex can be trained with equal success. Shepherds, whether male or female, are quick to learn, eager to please, and require a minimum measure of correction.

There is no appreciable difference between sexes in health care costs, providing your pup is spayed or castrated. If you are considering entering your German Shepherd in conformation classes (shows), it can't be neutered, and you must remember that females come in heat twice a year; thus you lose at least six weeks from each year if you are showing or involved with training classes. You can enjoy Tracking, Obedience, Herding, Agility, search and rescue, Frisbee, and 4-H competition with a spayed or neutered Shepherd.

Some of us appreciate the temperament of females; others prefer masculine characteristics. Male Shepherds, in general, tend to be larger and more aggressive than females, and this deserves consideration. Do you have other male dogs in the household? Another male might present a problem unless the males are raised together from puppyhood or are neutered, and even neutering won't necessarily stop male aggression. Females are usually more gentle than males, but this too is relative and varies among individuals. Shepherds live for training and work, thus the desire to please you in both work and play will dominate both sexes' personalities.

If you plan to show your German Shepherd Dog, do you also plan to raise puppies? If so, a show-quality female is your obvious choice. Few males are good enough to be considered stud dogs, and even if Duke wins his share of ribbons, he isn't likely to be in great demand for breeding.

Appropriate Age to Acquire a Puppy

From birth till about seven weeks of age, pups continuously learn nest etiquette from their dam and siblings. It is a serious mistake to remove them from this environment before they have fully absorbed the hands-on experience gained by interaction with other dogs.

Most breeders keep puppies until they are at least seven weeks old, at which

time they are given their first vaccinations, health exams, and worm check. Try to bring Duke home at or soon after that age. The critical human socialization period extends from shortly after birth to about three months of age. Pups should be introduced to humans as early as possible during this important bonding time. During this period, Duke will learn to trust his human family, and this trust will stay with him throughout his life.

Shepherds are often housebroken and have reasonably acceptable house manners by eight to twelve weeks of age. The period before twelve weeks is also the time when bad habits may be learned and those, too, are firmly imprinted in puppy minds.

If for some reason you aren't able to bring your Shepherd home before it is three months old, choose a puppy that has been properly and extensively handled by the breeder's family. Maturing without human companionship, having only other dogs with which to relate, may affect the pup's bonding with his new family; such a pup may prove to be a poor companion. However, German Shepherds are very human-oriented dogs. They will usually bond with an attentive family at any age if given enough love and care.

Finding the Right Breeder

Breeders can be located in a number of ways. Write to the AKC for the name of the current national or regional club secretary (see Useful Addresses and Literature, page 183). Ask for a list of club members in your locality. The AKC's web page may be accessed to find breed club secretaries and other information. The web address is http://AKC.org.

Dog Shows

To meet German Shepherd Dog fanciers, go to a dog show in your region. Attend Obedience trials, Herding tests, Agility, Tracking, and Frisbee contests. There you can meet people who will be invaluable if you are seeking a performance dog. Various dog magazines usually carry advertisements for German Shepherds. Information about shows and trials can be obtained from the *AKC Gazette*, a monthly publication of the American Kennel Club (see Useful Addresses and Literature, page 184). This publication also contains a breed listing with many kennels' advertisements.

A word to the wise. There are good and bad dog breeders just as there are good and bad pet shops. The number of litters whelped each year doesn't necessarily equate to the breeders' expertise or knowledge. Choose a breeder with a good reputation among his or her peers, and one who has produced winning dogs. Don't look only at the accomplishments of the dogs in the kennel, but how the puppies are handled.

Newspaper Ads

If you seek your German Shepherd through ads in your local newspaper, you may find trouble instead. Legitimate breeders may occasionally advertise in newspapers, but a backyard breeder who isn't interested in the betterment of the breed will often place a newspaper ad. Neighborhood litters offer a questionable source of companion dogs. Before you buy a backyard breeder's German Shepherd, be sure to examine the AKC registration and pedigree of the dam and sire. If the puppies aren't registered, or if their parents are less than two years old, beware! Backyard-bred puppies are often less expensive than kennel-raised dogs, and may prove to be fine companion dogs or pets, but it is unlikely you will receive conformation or performance guarantees of any kind.

Puppy Mills

Newspaper ads may promote Shepherds from puppy mills. Puppy factories or mills are establishments that maintain bitches of various breeds, and whelp hundreds of pups each year. They are notorious for mass-producing poor-quality pups with questionable health and parentage. Spotting a puppy factory is usually quite easy. When you arrive, a litter may be presented without the dam. If you ask to see her, an excuse is usually made, or if you do see her, she may be in questionable nutritional condition. If you gain admittance to the kennel, you will usually see various breeds, crowded, dirty conditions, very little provision for exercise, and thin, overworked dams. *Pups from puppy mills should be avoided at all costs.*

Pet Shops

Pet shops may be a viable option for you. They seldom have the dam or sire of a pup, and rarely can you see the puppy's siblings; however, many pet shops maintain pedigrees and complete records of the puppy's origin and you may learn the name of the kennel that raised the pup and thus satisfy your requirements. If the pup is AKC-registered, his pedigree can be obtained from them, but not usually before purchase.

What to Look For in a Pup

If you are looking for a healthy companion dog, and have no interest in formal training in Obedience, Herding, Tracking, or showing, making your selection will be easier. To assure that your pup is in good health, look it over from stem to stern before you buy it.

When confronted by a litter of happy, wriggling, tail-wagging puppies, it is difficult to concentrate on health issues, but it is important to do so before you choose a pup. Even a novice can inspect a pup and make a rough evaluation of his health, personality, and conformation to the Shepherd breed standard.

Look at Parents

If possible, look at both the pup's parents. Your pup is a genetic reflection of those dogs. If both have done well in shows, Tracking, or Obedience, you stand a good chance of their offspring having similar talents. If only the dam is present, ask to see a picture of the sire. If possible, ask to see pictures of his other progeny and his AKC-certified pedigree with annotations of his OFA certification number and other health certifications. Don't rule out a litter because of a dam's physical condition alone. A good Shepherd dam produces a fantastic amount of milk for her puppies, and may be nutritionally drained after six weeks of nursing. She may look a bit run-down after weaning a voracious litter of fat little Shepherd pups, have a saggy abdomen, be thinner than normal, with a dry and shedding coat. However, she should be clean, active, friendly, and inquisitive. Look at her puppies from previous litters if any are available.

Both parents should have been X-rayed and certified free of canine hip dysplasia (CHD) by the Orthopedic Foundation for Animals (OFA). Ununited anconeal process, or elbow dysplasia, is another hereditary fault often seen in German Shepherds. It can be identified by X-ray,

and certification of freedom from this disease may be provided by the OFA as well.

Health of the Pup

When you observe pups at weaning age, you won't be able to see every fault they possess, but you'll make a more intelligent choice if you follow these guidelines.

- You can't select a robust pup from a puny litter. If you see an assortment of skinny, runny-eyed, lethargic, coughing puppies, don't even pick one up. It's a mistake to take a sick pup home with the guarantee that he will get better in a day or two. Don't buy a puppy receiving medication. Wait until the therapy has been completed and a veterinarian has pronounced the pup healthy.

- Carefully observe the puppies' surroundings. If there are dirty food dishes lying about, overturned water bowls, and other signs of poor sanitation, beware! If the pups are confined to a yard, look for old feces on the ground or uneaten food attracting flies.
- Look at the puppy's eyes; they should be clear, not mattering or squinting.
- The nose rubber should be moist. Dry nostrils with matter caked in the corners are sure signs of health problems.
- The hind dewclaws (if any were there) should have been removed at about three days. Some Shepherd pups also have their front dewclaws removed, but it is optional.

Congenital and Hereditary Faults

After you have made friendly overtures to Duke for a few minutes while sitting on the floor, stand him upright on your lap. Open his mouth and check his bite. The upper incisor teeth should overlap and touch the lower front teeth. Any amount of gap between the upper and lower teeth (overshot or undershot) is a serious fault in Shepherds and should affect your choice, especially if you are looking for a dog to show or breed.

With Duke standing or sitting, feel his abdomen for evidence of umbilical hernia. A hernia may be identified as a soft protrusion of tissue under the skin, about the size of a marble, at the site of his navel. When the puppy is seven or eight weeks old, hernias are soft, and when pressed they may disappear into the abdomen. Hernias are easily surgically repaired, but they represent an additional expense to you.

If selecting a male, check for the presence of testicles. Both testicles should be descended into his scrotum by eight or ten weeks; if not, they may never descend. This hereditary defect doesn't present a serious problem in a companion animal or an Obedience or Tracking dog, but if you are considering entering Duke in dog show competition, either leave him with his breeder until both testicles drop into place, or choose another pup.

Shepherd pups eight weeks old should have sufficient cartilage strength in their ears to cause them to stand erect part of the time. Erect ears are mandatory for show dogs, but down ears can be tolerated in other competitions. Hanging ears rarely are seen when well-bred Shepherds are in good nutritional status.

Effect of hereditary faults. These congenital and sometimes hereditary defects may not cause the dog any difficulty. Most of them won't interfere with training, and a slight overshot or undershot jaw won't affect the nutrition of the dog. With the exception of hip and elbow dysplasia, and a few inherited ocular diseases, most of the common congenital defects discussed here aren't likely to shorten the life expectancy or decrease the quality of life of your Shepherd.

Temperament

It's often difficult to identify personality differences among puppies in a litter of playful, frisky youngsters. Temperament is critical when choosing a pup, especially

one destined for extensive training, and should be given appropriate attention.

The dam and sire will often give you a general idea of what their offsprings' attitude will be like when they grow up. Shy dogs usually don't make good companions, or at best they are more difficult to train and handle. Viciousness isn't typically a trait of Shepherds, but you should stay away from litters whose sire or dam is quarrelsome, belligerent, and difficult to handle. There is no excuse for buying a pup from a litter sired by, or born of, a dam with a bad attitude.

The Ideal Selection Process

Dog training begins when a pup is born, or within the first week of life. When humans handle newborn puppies, they are introduced to the human scent. Likewise, when a newborn puppy is exposed to the same human scent frequently, he will identify with that particular person's scent. After the pup is several weeks old, he will rely more on his eyes and ears as the major means of identification with humans.

Cooperative Breeders

If you are choosing a pup for a specific purpose—tracking for instance—you might ask the breeder to allow you to watch the litter from the time of birth. It isn't absolutely necessary to handle the pup at an early age, but, if possible, handling will help to imprint your particular scent on the mind of your future tracking partner.

You must realize that breeders of fine-quality German Shepherd Dogs may be reluctant to allow you this freedom, and certainly some restrictions should be placed on what you can and can't do with the puppy. If the breeder will cooperate, arrange to be introduced to the pup's dam long before the litter is born. You should visit her frequently during her pregnancy, petting her and bringing her small gifts of tasty morsels. With the owner's cooperation, you will be accepted and recognized as her friend before you try to handle her newborn pups. If your motives are pure and you back your proposal with a suitable down payment, you are more apt to find your plans approved by the breeder.

Assure the dam's owner that you will abide by all rules relative to cleanliness. Make sure you have not handled any other dogs before coming to see "your" pup. In addition, you should rub your hands on your armpits or bare feet before you handle the pup. This will intensify your scent, and he will become familiar with it before his eyes open. A loose bond will form between you and the pup if you expose him to your scent regularly. This bond will be strengthened if you can handle him a couple of times each week from birth until he is ready to leave his mother and siblings.

To choose your particular pup, you might watch the litter shortly after birth. Pick a puppy that is able to home in on a particular nipple at nursing time.

Even if you aren't successful in convincing the breeder to allow you to handle the puppy, by watching the litter from an early age you might be able to choose the pup showing curiosity about new odors and always finding his way back to the dam without crying. Such aptitude may be an indication of an excellent "nose" or capacity to concentrate on a particular odor. Puppies that have been chosen according to their early puppyhood abilities may continue to show extraordinary "nose" gift when they reach adulthood.

When the litter is three or four weeks old and allowed outside in the yard or in a large pen, you can watch the pups develop individual personalities.

- If a pup gets lost easily and whines until its mother comes to the rescue, it may not have the best scenting ability.
- If the pup wanders off, then retraces his steps to find his siblings and mother, that's a good sign.
- When he is a bit older, a Shepherd pup that notices crushed grasses and weeds in the yard and tends to follow such a trail with his nose is a good prospect for tracking work.
- Early signs of fetching and retrieving often indicate a good candidate. If these interests continue and increase as the pup nears weaning age, your selection may be made for you.

Picking Your Pup from a Litter

Don't frighten the puppies. Remember, you tower above the tiny pups, and your height alone is sufficient to cause apprehension.

- When you enter the room or yard where the puppies are housed, stand back and observe the litter from several feet away.

- Make a mental note of those not joining in the tumbling and play. Perhaps one or two will run and hide behind their dam or nesting box. Those pups are often insecure or poorly socialized, and are probably too young to leave their dam and siblings. Visit the litter more than once if all the pups seem shy; a few days at this age make a big difference.

- Sit or kneel down when interacting with the litter. Wad up a piece of paper, toss it across the floor, away from the puppies, and watch their reaction. If a particular pup always chases the paper first, make a note. You want a pup with good focus, one that will follow a ball or wad of paper and possibly retrieve it. If a pup watches you as you toss the paper wad, chases it, and brings it to you, mark that puppy well.

- Observe puppies that appear frightened when you clap your hands. Put a few marbles or pennies in a soda can and shake it behind your back, then roll it across the floor. A pup with confidence is one that twists his ears and looks around to see where the sound came from, then follows the can to investigate the noise. Such a pup could be a good selection.

- Puppies fleeing the instant a new sound is heard may not be the best training prospects. Timid puppies or those showing indifference to visitors are probably not good candidates for training.

- A pup that immediately takes a defensive stance when you reach for it should be rejected. If it snaps, screams, or otherwise seems frightened, it's probably not the pup for you. It may grow out of this attitude with time, training, and

socialization, but you should leave these chores to someone else.

- An overly aggressive puppy that is always involved in attacks on his siblings is a poor choice. Look for inquisitiveness and affection in your pup. A pup with a domineering or hostile attitude when playing with its littermates isn't likely to be the most easily trainable student.

- Try to concentrate on pups that are anxious to meet you rather than those hanging back; however, as a prospective trainee, you do not want a fireball. It is usually easier to increase the activity of a quiet pup than it is to slow down a hyperactive Shepherd.

- If a pup is curious about his visitors, but doesn't show any particular fear of them, put a plus beside that pup's name. If a puppy with many or all of the above qualities tries to follow you when you leave, your selection has been made.

After you have narrowed the selection process to one pup, sit on the floor and carefully pick Duke up. It is important to make yourself as small as possible when you first approach him. Lying down on the floor or lawn (if practical) is an excellent posture to take. Don't grab him as he runs by, and don't corner him somewhere. If the breeder's family has handled the pups, Duke will catch you; you won't have to chase him. Once selected, don't resist his active tongue. All his licking won't hurt you; it is his way of greeting you personally.

Take your chosen pup into another room away from the rest of the litter; sit on the floor and watch Duke's attitude when you set him beside you. If one end is wagging and the other is licking your face, you are nearing a good selection. Gently cradle him in your arms in an upside-down position and rub his tummy and chin. He should allow this attention with little objection and without immediately squirming to right himself. Such a pup is probably easily settled, and should be a good prospect.

After you have chosen Duke to be your pup, and before you take him home, ask the breeder to put an unwashed t-shirt, an unwashed sock, or some other item of yours with him for several days.

After you have obtained your Shepherd, watch Duke's actions when he encounters each new scent. While loose in your home or yard, place an item that has a concentration of another person's scent in front of him, and watch him carefully. If he sniffs it intensely, he may be a good candidate for obedience training and tracking.

Leave Duke in the backyard the next time you have friends in. Don't bring him indoors to greet them. After they've gone, bring him inside and watch to see if he sniffs and inspects each chair they used. Even at an early age, he can perceive other people's odors and distinguish them from those of his family. Fill Duke's world with a variety of new and different sights, scents, and sounds, but try never to let an experience "frighten" him. If you are training your pup to become a stock dog, introduce him at a young age to the livestock he will work. Carefully and gradually, bring him into the presence of sheep, fowl, and other farm animals.

Selection of a Pup for Special Training

Selecting a training prospect has been discussed to some degree already. The rule of thumb is: All purebred German Shepherds have the genetic background to allow them to compete in any of the sports for which the breed is eligible. However, if you have a special type of training in mind, look for a kennel raising pups from brood stock that do well in your sport. Some Shepherd breeders consistently win at Obedience; perhaps another kennel produces fine Tracking or rescue dogs. By contacting these kennels, you can hedge your bet a little, and will probably come up with a great Shepherd for the specialty you have chosen.

Show Dog/Training Prospect

If you want to show your dog in conformation classes, you should consider buying the pup from a kennel that produces show dogs. Most conscientious breeders can furnish a show and training prospect if you can afford the price. There is no difference between a "show kennel" and any other. Perhaps one or two pups from each litter from champion parents will attain championships. However, practically every puppy from the litter will be trainable, depending on the time you wish to spend in the training process. Ask show breeders about puppies with limited AKC registration. With these pups, you get showing rights, but your Shepherd can't be bred.

Companion Dog with Training

This is the category most of us would choose. We want an excellent pet, but one with the intelligence and aptitude to be trained and possibly compete. We aren't sure we will have the time or determination to train Duke to the competition level, but it's in the back of our minds, and we want a dog we can trust. This is the category of German Shepherd puppies most available. Pet-quality or companion Shepherds will provide more than enough

> A breeder's guarantee should cover replacement of puppy or monetary recompense for hereditary diseases that cannot be diagnosed until a later date. These include but are not limited to hip dysplasia and elbow dysplasia.

capabilities to satisfy the average owner. A pet-quality puppy from a kennel that raises show dogs will usually provide a respectable training prospect for most endeavors.

Health Records

What has health to do with training? Virtually everything! A pup in less than top nutritional condition and perfect health can't learn normally, and will never reach its full potential.

At last you have found the perfect puppy. Duke is a bundle of energy at playtime, and a sweetheart when he is cuddled. A number of documents should accompany your new German Shepherd. Among them are records of when and by whom the pup was vaccinated, the product used, and when another vaccination is due.

■ The date a worm check was done and the results of the fecal exam should be included, together with the date of treatment for the parasites if the fecal exam was positive. The health papers should specify what product was administered, the date, and the dose administered.

■ The records should include the dates of health examinations, and the name and address of the veterinarian who performed the exams.

■ If Duke was seen for an illness, it should be specified, as well as the name and dosage of medication used.

■ If heartworm, tick, or flea preventive medication has been started, the dates and the products used should be noted.

■ The pup's diet should be recorded, including the quantity, brand name, and frequency of feeding.

Breeders should have this information readily available, and usually more; be sure you receive it in writing. Continued preventive health care depends on complete health records.

AKC Papers and Guarantee

If the pup's parents are registered with the AKC, you should receive the puppy registration at the time you pay for and take Duke home.

A pedigree is a record of several generations of the puppy's ancestors, showing the various titles each of these dogs has attained. By itself, this paper has no particular value, especially if you are in the market for a companion or pet-quality pup. However, the titles of a pup's ancestors may be very significant if you have purchased a competition dog or if you

Sire's and dam's certified pedigrees that have OFA certifications are of great importance and will help in puppy selection.

intend to breed your Shepherd. Please note that a pedigree doesn't signify a great dog. A companion dog should be a good representative of the German Shepherd breed, regardless of whether or not it is a show- or breeding-quality pup.

Any special considerations that apply to the purchase should be put in writing. If you agree to spay or castrate the pup by a certain age, write it down. If the breeder guarantees the puppy to be in good health, get it in writing, together with the duration of the guarantee. Most breeders will replace a pup if it has a disease or deformity that is discovered by your veterinarian. Be sure the terms of the guarantee clearly specify whether it assures you of your money back, or a replacement pup.

Before You Conclude Your Purchase

Obligation and Dedication

Be sure you have time to spend with your new pet. Unfortunately, this point is frequently overlooked, especially if there are young children in the family. Grownups often make the mistake of delegating a puppy's care to a four- or five-year-old child; this is unfair to both child and puppy.

Do you have the necessary time to train a dog? Training isn't another "job" to do; it's relaxation and enjoyment, and should fit into your time schedule. If you can't spare this time, if it won't mesh with your current obligations, maybe you should re-think obtaining a puppy.

Necessary Facilities

Do you have physical space for a dog? In most cases, it includes at least a fenced yard and a warm, dry doghouse. Maybe a kennel and enclosed run will be needed to house Duke at certain times. Are these facilities within your budget? If the Shepherd pup is going to share your home, do you have a part of the yard to dedicate to Duke's toilet area? Do you have a spare room or a bathroom to help with housebreaking?

Are you frequently away from home? Have you investigated boarding kennels or do you have reliable friends who will care for your Shepherd when you are away?

Monetary Considerations

Can you afford a dog? The purchase price is only the beginning of dog ownership. There are annual vaccinations charges as well as neutering or spaying fees to consider. Every dog, even under the best circumstances, will occasionally require veterinary care. Call a veterinarian and get an average annual cost for medical maintenance.

Protection against ticks, fleas, and heartworm must be calculated. Your German Shepherd will deserve the best food. What will the cost be per year? Finally, consider the cost of dishes, beds, collars, and leashes.

Can you afford specialized training? If you plan to enter your German Shepherd in herding trials or any of the other competitions available to you, have you calculated the cost of a professional trainer,

training classes, equipment, and possibly handler's fees?

Do You Have the Necessary Patience?

Training is a labor of love, but it takes great patience. If you are quick-tempered or this is your first attempt to train, don't proceed before talking to several dog owners. Discuss the time they spend with their pets, because, at the very least, you must give Duke some home schooling and elementary obedience training. He must be taught good manners or he will be a liability rather than an asset.

4 *Understanding Training*

Rewards

People often approach every phase of training with a tidbit in their hands. When a particular exercise is performed satisfactorily, the dog is given a physical reward such as a bit of cooked liver or some other doggy treat.

Food rewards of this type may or may not enhance training. Treats may encourage learning by causing the dog to assume a desirable body attitude. At times, they are used simply to let Duchess know she has performed to your satisfaction.

In other instances, food rewards can distract from teaching or are superfluous depending on the particular task being taught. The Shepherd is known to be a people pleaser, a dog that will usually work for praise rather than treats. Duchess is likely to enjoy learning new things, and new experiences are often sufficient reward to maintain her enthusiasm, when coupled with vocal praise such as *"Atta girl."*

In most instances the training disciplines outlined herein can be taught without treats. If Duchess is strongly bonded to you, she will be happy to perform for your affection, which you must never fail to award with each success. Most German Shepherds live for their owner/handler. They will do amazing things, simply for a display of your approval, for your praise, and a little ear scratching. Duchess will

> **NOTE:** *In subsequent chapters, the "handler," a "friend," the "tracklayer," and the "victim" relate to people who are assisting in your training efforts. Gender-proper pronouns used for these people do not reflect sexism, and none is intended by the author. I've chosen to use masculine names and pronouns for the victim, tracklayer, and friend, and feminine names and pronouns for the owner and handler. This is done to avoid the clumsy use of "him or her," "his or hers," "he or she," and makes reading much easier.*
>
> *As you may have noticed in the last chapter, the hero of our book was a German Shepherd named "Duke." In this chapter, we will speak of a heroine called "Duchess." Duke and Duchess will take turns being the trainee. This is a technique designed to show that no sexism is ever intended.*

tidbit. If you have begun training with food rewards, try to phase them out as you move into more complicated tasks.

When *reward* is used in this book, unless stated otherwise, it means your approval. It means kind words, affectionate expressions, petting, scratching, and other displays of love, and occasionally, a treat.

First Things First

Your pup is now a reality. Duchess is home, busy sniffing around, introducing herself to all the interesting sights, smells, and sounds of your home. Where do you start?

One of the first things you must do is to encourage Duchess to *focus her attention on you*. Call her by name every time you meet her. Soon you will discover that she is monitoring your every move, listening for your voice.

Training begins the day your puppy arrives in your home. That doesn't mean you can start Duchess in search and rescue training or obedience classes at seven weeks old, but you will undoubtedly begin holding your puppy the first day. How can you resist?

work hard for the certain gentle voice modulation, which she will come to recognize as your ultimate approval. Your "*Good dog*," or "*Good girl*," will mean more to her than any tidbit.

If you wish to offer a performance reward, it should be very small and should be offered at odd times, not every time she does a task well. You should strive to never let her know when to expect the

Holding and cuddling a pup is most certainly a form of associative learning. Her first obedience lesson is taught when you pick her up and set her down at your convenience. Make this activity a happy time. When you pick her up, talk to her, pet and stroke her. She will squirm a little and prefer to be released. Releasing her is another reward, but she knows she must submit to being held if such treatment is your desire.

Associative Learning

Associative learning happens every day, as does the proof of your dominance, which must be firmly established quite early. When you groom her, she may try to escape, but you should quell her fears, and continue to brush her for a few minutes, talking to her all the while. After the grooming session is over, hold her while you pet her. She will associate grooming with the pleasurable experience of being caressed; she will realize you don't hurt her, and she must submit to you. It is critical for Duchess to learn very early who the pack leader is.

Anyone who says there is only one way to train a dog isn't thinking very well. If a dog has a certain personality trait or behavioral quirk, it's up to you to understand the idiosyncrasy, to think about it, and devise a way to make it work for you.

Any time Duchess comes to you, you naturally speak to her and pat her on the head. This establishes the fact that you like her to come, and when she does so, she is rewarded with praise and petting.

This thought should dominate your training throughout the life of the dog.

When Duchess does something you like, she receives your approval. That is the essence of training, from simple housebreaking to advanced Obedience work.

Praise the good and ignore the bad. Don't make a big display of some undesirable action of hers. If you do, she will remember how to get your attention, and may repeat the mistake whenever she feels neglected. Ignored or bored dogs will sometimes defecate on the sidewalk just to get your attention. They would rather be scolded than ignored.

German Shepherd Dogs are truly people-oriented and love interaction with their owners. If you continue training Duchess all her life, she will continue to respond and will appreciate your attention.

Mental Maturity

Like a human baby, a young puppy has cognitive ability at a very early age, and this capacity gradually increases throughout life. There is reason to believe that the more tasks and training a dog experiences, the greater will be her capacity to learn. Or to put it another way, it's possible when a dog is always on the learning curve, she never loses her propensity to learn new things.

Too many owners read this far and go no farther. Although dogs do think, reason, and have great intelligence, they can't verbalize their thoughts. They're unable to understand complex discussions; they are unable to comprehend abstract ideas. For this reason, you must establish communication with Duchess before anything else can go forward. This is done by gaining her focus at all times, and earning her confidence and trust. During the early stages of her training, she bonds with you

and establishes a reciprocal trust, a confidence that never ceases. She trusts you not to give her foolish commands or assign her tasks she can't perform. She trusts you to start her in the right direction, and keep her on the right track. She learns you will always reward her with your love and approval for a job well done.

You begin to trust Duchess very early as well. As you progress with her housetraining, you develop confidence that she won't mess in the house. You may next trust her not to chew up the garden hose. As she matures a bit more, you have faith she will behave around other dogs. Your reciprocal trust in Duchess grows by leaps and bounds throughout her life. Trust is enhanced by your continued willingness to work with her and reward her.

Pack Mentality

From day one, she looks to you as the pack leader who gives her jobs to do and who rewards her when they are done correctly. She also comes to you to play and to receive your love, even when she has done nothing more to earn it than to offer her love. Her principal desire is to please you.

Your Role as Pack Leader

You should expand on this pack mentality to establish your role as pack leader.

■ When she is still a puppy, sit on the floor and hold her quietly but firmly in front of you and massage her back, neck, ears, chest, and muzzle. When she squirms to free herself, keep her in position for several more minutes, and release her when she has relaxed and is not trying to get away. Once she sees that you are stronger than she is and are not about to give up on this task, she will appreciate the massage. Repeat this every day or twice a day.

- Demonstrate your dominance and leadership by making Duchess move out of your way when you walk from room to room. Physically remove her from your chair or her favorite place in the room, and take her place.
- If she eats in the house, feed her after you have eaten, and don't tolerate begging at your table.
- Ignore her occasionally when you come home and reserve your affection for a few minutes later.
- When playing tug-o-war with her, win the game at least half the time, and when you have won, put the toy away, out of her sight.
- Keep all her favorite toys out of her reach, and give one to her as a special treat. Don't allow her on your bed or in the bedroom except when she is specifically invited.
- Occasionally tie her in the yard while you are busily working around her.
- If you find yourself with a rather aggressive or domineering puppy, handle her frequently and extensively. Touch every part of her body, including her paws, tail, belly, muzzle, and back. Open and examine her mouth, look into her eyes for a second. Hold her mouth shut for a minute. Rub her ears, talk in a soothing manner, and repeat her name time and again.

- Frequently turn Duchess on her back while you rub her tummy and stretch her legs, first one then another. Have every member of your family get into the touching program. If you continue this type of handling all her life you will be rewarded when you begin serious training, because Duchess will accept you as the pack leader, and will take a subservient role in the family.
- As Duchess matures, make a point of taking up her food bowl while she is eating; take her for a walk around the yard, then let her continue eating.
- Teach her to come and to sit very early in life. Be sure those two commands are always promptly obeyed, and if

necessary, teach them for five or ten minutes every day or even twice a day. This will further establish your dominance over her and fortify your role as pack leader. If you intersperse this routine with lots of love and petting, you will produce a more trainable dog. Give Duchess gentleness and respect, and earn hers by fair treatment.

Each of these ideas, and others you may devise, should be practiced regularly to let her know she is loved, but you are the leader and will always call the shots.

Trainability and Intelligence

These two terms are interrelated, but their meanings are not identical. The Shepherd as a breed has been proven to be highly intelligent, but is intelligence alone what we want?

Trainability

Trainability is a measure of a dog's ability to learn, her desire to learn, her desire to please her master, or the ease with which she takes direction. It is associated with personality, which is partly genetic and partly learned. A dog that is bonded to you and dependent on you will more likely be anxious to gain your approval. *Dependence* and *focus* are personality traits often considered the most important features of a highly trainable dog. If Duchess has a relatively low level of kinetic energy, is patient and receptive, and is focused on you, looking to you for direction, she is apt to be an exceptional training prospect. If you encourage her dependence on you throughout her training, you will enhance her trainability.

If your puppy is quite active, has a high energy level, intense curiosity, and extreme intelligence, you will probably have some difficulty channeling her actions to productive training.

Personality tests are sometimes given to puppies at about seven weeks, and are a fairly reliable guide for prospects destined for training in a particular discipline. Testing is done by a third party, someone who is not acquainted with the pup, and in a location away from the pup's home. These tests use a number of props, and may help you choose between two or three available puppies. If you are interested in such testing, contact a local all-breed dog club or ask your veterinarian.

Intelligence

Intelligence relates to a dog's problem-solving ability. Intelligence is manifested by Duchess's attitude toward seemingly impossible situations. If she is faced with an 8-foot (2.4-m) brick wall and wants to get to the other side, she may elect to use a ladder propped against the fence.

Another example of canine intelligence is the guide dog whose master is a 6-foot (1.8-m) man. She measures his height, and refuses to take him under an awning hanging lower than his height. This is not training; it is a display of inherent intelligence.

In the best of all worlds, exceptional intelligence will be coupled with a highly trainable personality.

Ability to Understand

Set realistic goals. Dogs are capable of understanding more than you realize, but don't expect too much of Duchess. Ability increases with experience, association, concentration, and repetition. German Shepherds are bright creatures, and when Duchess hears a sound (a particular word or command), she should recognize the sound and associate it with her subsequent activity.

This is not to claim that dogs have cognitive abilities equal to those of human beings. Probably they are unable to reach any significant level of abstract reasoning, but Duchess has an excellent memory, and rarely will "forget" a particular activity once it is grasped and filed in her memory bank.

If you are careful to keep your commands simple and distinct, and always connect the word with the same activity, Duchess's understanding and vocabulary will be increased day by day. Don't confuse her. Give her short, concise, explicit commands on which she can concentrate, and thus understand. Never give her a command for a task she is physically or mentally incapable of performing. Early in any training, make her tasks simple, gradually increasing the difficulty as she grasps the simple endeavors.

Two-way Communication

Patience and careful observation will lead you to appreciate Duchess's signals. You must watch for her signs of understanding. Her body language, facial expression, tail carriage, and limb movement all have meanings. You will learn to tell when she is processing your command in her mind and deciding how to do the task you have given her. Her response to your command is twofold: She will tell you she understands what you ask, then she will obey. As you begin to interpret her body language, you will be able to assist her when she is puzzled. Perhaps she needs a bit of physical help or a further word from you.

When you have learned to understand and respond to her, you have dog training nearly conquered. You can't teach the dog; you can only lead her to learn what actions you expect from her. The more time you spend working and playing with your dog, the greater the bond you will enjoy. The more attention and focus she gives you, the better she will respond.

Readiness to Learn, and Work-Play Balance

Shepherds are as ready to learn as you are to instruct. You can preserve and perpetuate this readiness by giving short lessons.

Dog massage is a new technique that is said to aid training, prepare a dog for physical activities, and improve canine health in general. A center for teaching, presenting seminars, and furnishing information and videos is the Institute for Canine Massage. Information is available on the Internet at www.dogmassage.com.

Take care not to bore or tire Duchess at any stage of training. Endless repetitions of a particular activity are counterproductive. All puppies' attention span is quite short, and the lesson should be kept even shorter. Repeat your first lesson two or three times, then quit.

For example, it might take a minute or two to give eight-week-old Duchess a lesson to come. This lesson should be repeated no more than three times in a single session, then take time out, play with her; it's recess time and school is out. Take her for a walk to change the subject. If you can repeat the *come* session three times each day, so much the better, but never stay with something "until she learns it." Such an attitude will only tire and bore her.

If you have the time and patience, when one session and a time of play is completed, you can introduce another elementary lesson. For example, teach hide-and-seek. *Come* and hide-and-seek exercises have totally different concepts, and she probably will enjoy both of them. By switching from one to another, Duchess is less apt to become a weary and bored student.

Almost Right Is Still Wrong

Remember, a reward is anything Duchess likes, whether it is a pat on the head, a scratch under the ear, a kind word, or a special tidbit from your hand.

Almost right is still wrong. Never reward her for *trying*, or she will never get it right. When an exercise is not done

Clicker Training

Sometimes a clicker is used by a trainer to signal her dog that the task has been performed properly. In other words, the clicker is substituted for a personal, verbal "Atta-girl" or "Good dog." A clicker-trained dog quickly learns that a reward will be offered when she hears the distinctive, metallic sound. However, ethics are sometimes breached when an owner, handler, or someone in the gallery stands outside the ring and uses a clicker indiscriminately. The click-click will distract a competing clicker-trained dog that is performing. Clickers all sound alike. The competing dog may be confused, or she may misfire and ruin her chances for a smooth performance. Consider that possibility if you are (were) planning to use a clicker to train your performance dog. You might want to return to the time-honored signal that is unique and meaningful for your dog, your voice!

correctly, simply change the subject. Don't scold her or make a big issue of her failure. Instead, when she fails, just pick up her leash and take her for a walk. Forget the lesson for a day and spend a few minutes with her in an exercise she has already learned.

Any time your dog is confused by or uncomfortable with a particular exercise, STOP. Reconsider where you are. Build her confidence by asking her to do a task she has mastered. Forget the new one for a few days, then try introducing it again. When you reintroduce the task, if she tries but still is unable to understand, don't condemn her but don't reward her either. Begin another much simpler task, one she can easily understand, then heap praise on her when she gets it right.

It is important for Duchess to succeed and receive a reward at the end of each training session, but not necessarily for each task.

Her failure is probably due to her lack of understanding of what you want accomplished. When dealing with failures, you must accept at least half the blame, and try to devise a better way to teach the task.

Once Duchess completely understands what her job is, her desire to please will lead her to success. If Duchess is a typical Shepherd, she will amaze you with those successes.

Bonding with Trainer-Handler

Typical Shepherds are born with the desire to please their owners. They are naturally giving and responsive dogs. Your job is to perpetuate this desire to please. When a task is successfully completed, give Duchess lots of praise and show her your approval.

Affection between the handler and the dog can't be faked. If you love your dog, you will show it. If you treat Duchess fairly, and demonstrate your love at all times, she will bond with you like glue; however, bonding is rarely exclusive.

She may show similar affection for your spouse, your children; even some acquaintances may be taken into her circle of friends. Bonding with other friends is not the same as her association with you. Her ties are strongest to the person with whom she spends the most productive time, with her mentor, her teacher.

A Shepherd's inventive mind needs to be kept busy. Duchess will appreciate the time you spend with her, whether it is in play or teaching her some trick or task. By the same token, you will appreciate her, her talents, and her learning ability more each time you work with her.

Establishing Trainee and Trainer Roles

Dominance was mentioned earlier but needs to be reiterated. Never leave any doubt about who is in charge. The collar is around Duchess's neck, and the leash is in your hand. You are the teacher, and Duchess is the student. These roles must be honored, and you should take care not to allow her to reverse them.

If you have obtained an adult Shepherd and attempt to teach her something she resents or will not immediately perform, take her for a walk on her leash. Then, instead of starting with an exercise she *should* be able to do, start with something you know she *can* do, such as *fetch*, *come*, or *sit*. When she performs the task correctly, lavish praise on her. Play catch with her, toss her Frisbee, or simply show her affection for coming to you. Eventually, reintroduce the problem exercise.

Discipline, Force, and Punishment

These three words can have similar meanings and are often used synonymously, but their interchangeable use is fraught with problems.

Discipline

Discipline is sometimes defined as training, and in another place, it means chastisement or punishment. It can mean control, or it may refer to the rules imposed in a learning endeavor. Think of discipline as training, resulting in development of self-control. In other words, discipline is a necessary part of training your German Shepherd, and without it she isn't apt to learn anything more difficult than her name. *Discipline is not physical punishment or verbal abuse.*

A well-disciplined dog can be trusted to perform in a certain way under certain circumstances. In order to accomplish this, the teacher must always dominate the dog during training. You, the handler, must make your will the dominant feature of your association with Duchess, but you must accomplish this without abuse.

Force

Force is another word you may encounter when reading training literature. It's sometimes necessary to use force in training, but it's rarely thought of as such. In training, force may have nothing to do with pain or abuse. You must be able to weigh the value of the use of force against the adverse results that occur when it is used. Always keep your temper under control, be consistent, and persevere. There are several elements of force implemented in practically all training.

Restraint is a type of force and should be taught to a puppy or an adult dog at the very beginning. In a pack, a puppy's submissive body attitude is characterized by rolling over on its back, exposing its tender belly to a superior dog. When you picked up Duchess for the first time, you turned her on her back and rubbed her tummy and chest. This is a type of force. She was too small to object strenuously, and you forced your will upon her.

As you continue to roll your Shepherd on her back during her puppyhood and into adulthood, you might not think of it as force, but it is. When you manipulate her legs, rub her feet, and make her sit, those are all forces you impose on her.

Sit has been said to be the most important obedience command you can teach your dog. It is not instinctive for a dog to sit on command. It is a learned behavior. By forcing Duchess to sit whether she wants to or not, you are causing her to do something beyond her instinctive habits.

While in a training mode, you should never give Duchess a command you can't enforce. Take care not to put her into situations where her actions are arbitrary and she can easily disobey. When she is a puppy, and you tell her "*Sit*" when you are too far away to cause her bottom to touch the ground, Duchess may elect to remain standing. This constitutes a negotiation on her part, and puts you, the trainer, in an untenable situation. An inexperienced trainer will waste breath on repeated commands, and finally may resort to yelling "*SIT*" at the top of his voice, probably with repeated negative results.

Punishment

Punishment usually refers to negative reinforcement of a command or a negative human reaction to a canine action. It is used by some trainers as a means to dissuade a dog from repeating an incorrect response to training, and its use is a judgment error in most instances.

Example: Duchess makes a mistake when told to heel, so the handler jerks her leash, and the training collar snaps her neck. The next time Duchess is given the same command, she will remember the collar snap, and will be thinking about her sore neck instead of an appropriate response to the command. Her caution when she subsequently hears the command causes a delay in response and brings about a firmer yank on the leash and a vocal reprimand from the handler. This handler reaction makes the dog afraid to do anything when the command is given, and she slides backward in her training.

A gentle tightening of the training collar without a word being spoken has a much more lasting effect on Duchess than yelling, nagging, or jerking the collar.

Verbal "correction" can be a form of punishment or abuse when it is frequently repeated, especially when it is joined with a physical action. Have you ever eavesdropped over a backyard fence when a neighbor is training his dog? Every other word is "*No,*" often followed by a verbal tirade no dog could ever hope to understand.

Inappropriate discipline, force, or punishment may cause Duchess to shun training by running from you, or avoid you by any means she can devise. At this point, bonding is impossible.

Methods of Training

There are four techniques routinely used in training.

1. The first and, in most dogs, the best method is to bond so well with your

wonderful sense of smell to your verbal command. A pat on the head, a scratch behind the ears, and a "*Good girl*" should be the only reward she expects. Such response should always be your goal, although there are situations where the second method may be added for greater success and quicker response.

2. The second method is to make Duchess realize that each time she responds appropriately she will receive a tasty reward. To use this method, you are required to always keep tidbits in your pocket, and you give her a yummy every time she obeys and performs according to direction. This method is most applicable in exercises such as *sit*, *down*, *heel*, and several of the little tricks mentioned. These are not extensions of natural instinctive actions; they are arbitrary tasks we have devised to make the dog more acceptable in human society.

3. The third method is the force method, in which every command is impressed by enforcement using human reactions. This is usually counterproductive and is rarely needed when training your German Shepherd.

4. The fourth and most logical method is a combination of the three depending on the situation. Keep in mind "force" is a relative term, and any force must be carefully thought out before it is employed.

dog that she will listen and respond to you, expecting nothing more than your praise and petting as rewards for her successes.

Praise, in voice and action, is most successful when the task being taught is an extension of the dog's natural instincts. For example, teaching *find* is nothing more than relating Duchess's

The most important thing to remember about training is to get and hold Duchess's attention. Without her unceasing focus on you and your commands, you're spinning your wheels.

Basics

The initial thought in the very simplest training must begin with you and what your reaction is when Duchess does something. If she happily comes to you and jumps on your leg affectionately and playfully, and in the process, tears your clothes, what is your reaction to be? Think about it. She came to you—how can you reprimand her for such action?

Your messages to Duchess must be loud and clear and easily understood. Furthermore, they should be only positive reactions. How do you accomplish such a chore? Surely she must be disciplined for jumping up; you can't tolerate the action—how can you respond positively to a negative action? The answer to this and other questions follows in the next chapter, on manners.

Communication

Even young puppies have the capacity to think, reason, and plan. They are equipped with fantastic memories and certainly understand human sounds (words), if we keep the words we use short, crisp, and meaningful. Duchess can't carry on a subjective conversation, and she can't be expected to know what you're thinking. She is confused by multiple commands having different or complex meanings.

She can communicate with us if we are bright enough to interpret her sounds and body language. Duchess will routinely display loyalty, protectiveness, grief, and joy. How do dogs learn? Since they haven't the ability to read or understand complex statements, and their

capacity for abstract thinking is probably poor, we must use some fundamental tools.

Associative Learning

Associative learning is a type of learning relating an action to a reaction. The simplest type of associative learning is when Duchess behaves and you pet her. She does something and you react to it immediately. She connects her action (behaving) to your reaction (petting).

Duchess correlates a reward she receives for a particular desirable action she performs on command. The reward may be an edible treat, or preferably a kind word, a pat on the head, or scratching behind her ears.

Human socialization is an example of inherent behavior coupled with associative learning. As a pup, Duchess discovers that handling and

petting feels good; thus her innate desire to please is supported or reinforced by her experience, and she cultivates a lifetime bond with her owner. She learns her owner's responses to her performances are food, warmth, grooming, petting, and play. By associating these physical rewards with a human, she becomes socialized.

Associative learning may also be negative. This is seen when Duchess performs inappropriately and as a result meets with an unpleasant sensation, which is usually painful or frightening. Duchess's mother initiated this type of learning when she snapped at the puppy for grabbing her tail. Duchess must learn that her inappropriate behavior, at the very best, leads nowhere and gets her nothing.

Negative Reinforcement

Strong negative reinforcement or negative association has been proven to be an undesirable and often ineffective technique to use in dog training. Hitting the dog if she doesn't obey a command is an example of negative association. Yelling "*No*" at the top of your voice or throwing something at her is another example of inappropriate negative reinforcement. When she is seen digging in the garden, call her to you and play catch with her until she has forgotten her previous activity. Negative reinforcement techniques are not only inadvisable, they are usually inhumane, may be counterproductive, and often interfere with your ability to teach the dog anything.

Sometimes mild *remote* negative devices such as squirt guns or spray bottles can be used in training under certain circumstances.

Example: Duchess insists on getting on the furniture when you are out of the room. You don't want her there, but she never happens to jump on the couch when you are in the room, and if you aren't present, it's impossible to stop her. Direct a stream of water at her through the crack of a door where you can't be seen. She may associate the water with jumping on the sofa, not with you, in which case she will probably remember the experience and refrain from repeating the action.

Habituation

Learning can also be accomplished by habituation, which means Duchess becomes accustomed or conditioned to a given incident or situation.

Habituation is the type of learning that allows a guide dog to perform in heavy, noisy traffic in the city. It is especially important with military and police dogs that must be conditioned to the noise of gunfire. This type of learning uses the dog's intelligence and experience, which adds to her instinctive behavior.

Although the various training is discussed here in steps, beginning when Duchess is a weanling puppy, actual training occasionally may jump ahead. For instance, one of the earliest commands she will learn is *come*, or *here*, which is an obedience command, but one you will undoubtedly teach long before obedience training begins. Duchess will associate *come* or *here* with being called to a meal, to play, and many other events. Leash

training will occur at the same time she is being housetrained, and the various play sessions begin very early as well.

Remember, learning is cumulative. It is the sum of all the knowledge Duchess may pick up through experience or by accident, as well as by the conscious effort of her instructor. Consistency is therefore of the utmost importance.

Playtime

Before discussing any specific training, a word about play. Playing with Duchess is as important as any lesson you can teach. Never forget to take time out from training, or to skip training altogether some days, just to play with her. As you will see later, play can be constructive teaching, but Duchess won't know it. Play might be defined as any activity your dog really appreciates, an activity she truly enjoys.

The younger the pup, the shorter the attention span. Don't expect Duchess to see into the future. She wants to play all the time, but she will enjoy being with you and getting your attention. If every training session is followed by a play period, both owner and dog will be happier.

5 *Manners and Housetraining*

Manners

Manners might be defined as social conduct that agrees with prevalent human customs. Good manners are acceptable characteristics or deportment a dog displays when he is in a human environment. Manners reflect the learned behavior of dogs when in homes, whether yours or your neighbors'. Appropriate manners are essentials, and should be taught to all dogs.

The German Shepherd has an instinctive desire to please, which has been established through the breed's long association with humans. The greatest reward Duke receives is the approval of his owner. A pat on the head, a scratch behind the ears, a kind word, gentle handling, an occasional treat; these comprise the salary for which Duke works. The aspiration to please, plus the Shepherd's innate mentality, reasoning ability, and natural behavior make him an ideal house companion with a minimum of training.

Manners aren't usually considered a part of training. When we think of training a dog, we usually review Obedience work, Tracking, or other more advanced education. Learning good manners begins the day he comes into your home and doesn't end for many years.

The tools to use at this stage of elementary training are repetition, substitution, prevention, and positive reinforcement. Teaching manners is nothing more than simple behavioral modification. The same teaching tools will be used when Duke is subjected to advanced, complex training sessions readying him for Obedience, Tracking, or Herding trials. The difference is that Duke is now just a puppy with a very short attention span and limited understanding. His age and lack of experience are his major barriers to complicated instruction.

Any training attempts for puppies should be kept simple. The commands must be simple, and Duke's responses will be simple. Be sure he fully understands what is expected of him in every case. Don't reprimand him for mistakes he makes. Above all, keep your temper and have patience. Remember Duke's background— a few days ago his only encounters with the world took place in his nest with his dam and siblings. Nest deportment is significantly different than the manners we are now about to require of him.

Duke, Come

The first thing Duke is to learn is his name, and the second is the *come* command. He will respond to his name upon hearing it frequently, and *come* will easily be taught as well.

Take advantage of his natural responses. In other words, step outside, where the pup is playing. As soon as he looks at you, call his name. If he begins to run toward you, tell him *"Come."* If he doesn't, pick up his food bowl, and the instant he begins to come toward you, tell him *"Come."* When the pup arrives, praise him with excitement and exuberance. Build confidence in the pup. Give him the impression that his response is always right.

To reinforce the *come* command, fasten a long, lightweight nylon line to Duke's collar. Allow him to wander away from you for some distance, then, with zeal, drop to one knee and give the command, *"Duke* (hesitation), *come."* If he doesn't respond with the enthusiasm you expect, give a tug on the line, repeating the command once. When Duke arrives on your lap, lavish praise on him and tell him what a good dog he is. Then release him from the exercise with an *"OK,"* and continue to praise him.

Repeat this exercise frequently at odd times to catch him off guard. When his response to the command has become automatic, try him off leash, in the fenced yard. Repeat the command several times daily for grooming, feeding, and especially for petting, but never call Duke to you to scold or discipline. That will defeat your purpose. Instead, each time he comes on

The come command is mentioned dozens of times throughout this book. It is perhaps the easiest command to teach your puppy and can be used in many everyday situations and games. You will probably teach Duke to come at feeding time, and he won't realize what you are doing. This is one exercise easily learned by a very young pup, and the sooner it is mastered, the better. It should be practiced frequently, until Duke's response is automatic.

command, praise and pet him, regardless of what mischief you have called him from.

Housetraining

"All training of the dog should be on the theory he is a reasoning animal, possessing keen perception of cause-and-effect in connection with the circumstances which are within the scope of his animal needs, domestic life, and every-day observation." This is a quote taken from B. Waters' book, *Fetch and Carry*, published in 1895. It is as true today as it was over a century ago.

In the first few weeks of life, Duke did whatever he felt like doing. If he had the urge to chew on his bed, no one told him not to. If he felt like eating, there was probably food to be had or his mother was available to nurse. If he had the urge to urinate, he did so without any self-incriminating thoughts. Defecation was another natural urge he attended to without regard to his timing or where he happened to be standing. This was his world and those were the behavioral rules by which he lived. Then, one day you selected him and carried him from this perfect milieu to the restrictive environment of your home. His natural behavior didn't suddenly change because of his place of residence, but now, rather suddenly, he finds he must modify his manners. How can he do it? How can you expect a sudden change in his demeanor?

Conditioning the Thinking Process in Your Pup

Duke must be made to think, and to think in relation to cause and effect. That's your job, to bring about the thinking process in your puppy. To a pup, urinating isn't a mistake; it's natural. To housetrain Duke, you must impose human restrictions on his life. You must cause him to "think" like a human. He has no way of knowing about human customs until he is taught; therefore, you should never punish, scold, or otherwise reprimand him for messing on the floor.

Young puppies use little discretion, and when they feel the urge to urinate or defecate, they hardly hesitate a second. The job is finished before you notice, then it's too late to correct. Dog trainers have estimated that for effectiveness, your response to a puppy's accident must take place within five seconds from the time the accident occurs, after which time the puppy will not associate his action with any corrective measure you may take.

If you swat Duke when he is performing a natural act, you will confuse him. Rubbing his nose in his urine is equally confusing to the pup, isn't likely to make a lasting impression on him, and might even damage his sensitive nose. Once the natural act of urination or defecation is begun, it's already gone from the puppy's mind.

Consider what you're about: You are taking a weanling puppy, seven or eight weeks old, and teaching him an entirely new set of behavioral rules. It seems an impossible task, but in reality it is quite easy, because you are only enlarging on instincts prevalent in all canines. Adult dogs are clean animals. In the feral state, their toilet areas are far from their dens. They don't soil their beds or sleep next to their excretions. While in the nest, their dam immediately cleans up after them.

- After he has emptied his bladder or bowels in the toilet area, praise him, play with him, and allow him back inside.
- Always take Duke to this special toilet area of the yard for his eliminations. When the odors of previous eliminations are established in the special area, he will seek out the spot regardless of where he is or what he is doing.
- Take him to the toilet area immediately following each meal, when he cries at night, as soon as he wakes in the morning, after naps, and before bedtime at night. If you are able to train yourself to this task, Duke will be housetrained before you know it.

Nighttime Training

A good rule is to take away Duke's food and drinking water two hours before his bedtime. Sometimes a walk before bedtime will encourage sleeping, and don't forget to take him to his toilet area immediately before he turns in for the night.

Buy him a large or extra large crate (kennel), one that is large enough for an adult Shepherd to stand and turn around in. German Shepherds are big dogs and the crate has many uses. The crate should be made of fiberglass. It should have ventilation apertures on three sides and a positive-locking metal gate on the front. It should be of the type used to ship dogs by air and not the collapsible wire confinement type. Otherwise, Duke could chew it and injure his mouth.

Place Duke in his crate containing an old sweater or some other article with

Technique

Begin on the day Duke makes his appearance in your home.

- When you see him preparing to urinate or defecate on the floor, don't scold him, yell at him, or make a big fuss as he prepares to eliminate on the carpet. Doing so will only prolong his housetraining time.
- Instead, pick him up immediately and take him to a particular area of the backyard, place him on the ground, and slowly back off. At first, he will be confused, but if you put him in the same area each time, he will soon realize it is the place for his eliminations.

> **NOTE:** *The rawhide bones and other chewies made from a single piece of untanned leather have occasionally been incriminated as the cause of gastrointestinal blockage in some dogs. This becomes a problem when the dog chews off a piece and swallows it whole. When we speak of rawhide chewies in this book, we refer to chew sticks made of small pieces of rawhide pressed into many shapes.*

your scent, his nylon chew bone, and nothing else. He will object to this confinement, but if you give him a little favor, perhaps a rawhide chewy, he will soon accept the restriction. If he cries, don't scold him; simply walk away.

During the night, you must train yourself to tend to him immediately when he cries. You do so by taking him from his crate and carrying him to the toilet area of the yard. Don't play with him, pet him, or make a fuss over him in any way; this is a duty trip only. If he defecates or urinates, praise him. Return him to his crate after a few minutes in the toilet area, whether he has eliminated or not. Your first duty in the morning must be to take him again to the toilet area.

Before you know it, your nighttime trips to the backyard are past history, and the door to his kennel can be left open. You will no longer need to carry him to the toilet area; when you open the back door, he will zoom to it on his own. When Duke feels the urge during the daytime,

he thinks about it, and whines at the back door. You have altered his behavior by conditioning. His urge to eliminate is associated with a specific place.

Doggy Door. If your backyard is securely fenced, you can now equip your back door with a doggy door he can use any time, but be sure to buy one that will accommodate Duke when he is an adult. Usually, adult dogs can hold their eliminations through the night. A doggy door is a convenience for Duke; it will sometimes save you steps, but it is not a necessity.

Housetraining Summary

Repetition (or consistency), prevention, substitution, and positive reinforcement are the most reliable tools to use when housetraining your pup.

- Be consistent; when Duke asks to go outside, *repeat* your actions and don't deviate from them.
- Confine the pup; never let him out of your sight when he is indoors. In that way you can quickly *prevent* him from messing on the floor.
- When he shows signs of turning in circles in preparation for moving his bowels, pick him up quickly and *substitute* the toilet area of the yard for your carpet.
- When he complies and deposits his eliminations in the appropriate place, *praise and reward* him.

To housetrain a pup, great patience is required, and persistence will pay off.

If you wish to try a door bell, you will probably find it easy to train Duke to use it. Hang a bell on a thong from the doorknob on the inside and outside of the back door. When he whines at the door to go outside, ring the bell with his paw, then open the door for him. Do the same thing when he whines to come into the house. The door bell isn't really a necessary accessory, but it may save paint on the door, and it adds a bit of flair to his training. Don't forget the reward when he performs correctly.

Don't expect miracles. After Duke is housetrained, he may occasionally still have an accident. Don't lose your temper. His attention span is short but his memory is great. Once he fully understands what is expected of him, he will try to please you.

Paper Training

Teaching your Shepherd to urinate or defecate on newspapers is possible but not recommended. Paper training may look good to you when there is fresh snow on the lawn in the backyard, and when Duke is a seven-week-old furry little puppy, but remember, if you use this method of housetraining, eventually you will want to teach Duke to put his rather copious stools and puddles in the backyard, not on newspapers on the kitchen floor.

Technique

If paper training is desirable—for example when you can't be with your pup—put Duke in a portable pen in a bathroom or other easily cleaned, tiled room. Cover one-half the floor of the pen with several layers of newspaper, and place his nylon bone, water dish, and bed on the other half. He now has no choice but to use the newspapers for his eliminations. After a week or two, you can remove the pen, but keep him confined to the small room with the newspapers on the floor when you are not with him. In all probability, he will continue to use them, and within a reasonable time, he can be trusted to roam over the house and still return to the papers for eliminations.

Paper training doesn't resolve the housetraining chore; it just prolongs it. This training may confuse the naturally clean Shepherd by forcing him to defecate beside his food and bed.

Apartment Living

Shepherds, being very clean dogs, can easily adjust to apartment dwelling. This arrangement requires a bit more effort from the owner, but can be accomplished with a little planning. While Duke is still a puppy, follow the directions given for paper training, but never fail to take him for frequent excursions outside.

When Duke first arrives in your apartment, begin a regular "walk" routine and establish a relationship to his toilet area. Take him outside to the designated walking place at every opportunity, but no less than the first thing every morning, the last thing every night, and at least twice during the day. This walking place might be a park if one is nearby. If you are limited to using a city sidewalk or alley, be sure he recognizes that defecation and urination must be accomplished in the gutter, not on the sidewalk.

When using the gutter as his toilet area, the same general rules apply as previously discussed. Praise and petting are used to encourage appropriate response. The differences are, he must empty his bowels and bladder while on a leash, and you must carry some provision to pick up and remove his solid waste as it is deposited. Buy a supply of cheap disposable plastic gloves and bags for this purpose, or a more elaborate pooper-scooper and bucket can be used.

Crate Training

Think of Duke's crate or kennel as his den, his place of refuge. One of the first commands to teach Duke when he arrives in your home is *kennel*, or *crate*, which means he is to go into his crate and stay there.

Never use crating as a punishment for some mischief he has gotten into; always make his association with his crate positive. Give him praise when he enters his crate, as well as a chew stick, nylon bone, or other treat. Put an article of your unwashed clothing in the crate; he will recognize your scent and will be more comfortable. Most dogs enjoy the cavelike atmosphere of a crate when sleeping, and a crate often makes a dog a welcome guest in motel rooms when you are traveling.

While Duke is still a puppy, crate him several times daily for short periods. Once he has been put in the crate, tell him *"Wait,"* then walk away and don't turn back. Don't spend any time telling him good-bye, just close the gate and beat a rapid retreat, ignoring his pleas to follow. Once he has settled down and accepted his confinement for a while, let him out and praise and play with him for a few minutes.

A quick spray of water will be sufficient to correct nuisance behavior indoors.

The *wait* command may also be used to let him know he is to stay in a particular place and await your return. It differs from the obedience command *stay* in that he is not expected to remain in a particular position, but must simply trust you to return to him. It may be used when leaving him in a car, boarding kennel, veterinary office, tied in the yard, or any other temporary place.

The kennel or crate can also be used to shut him away on occasion from attractive kitchen odors. He will voluntarily use this den for napping or to escape the activity of the household when it becomes hectic or irritating. It will soon be one of his favorite places, quiet and secluded.

Totally Confining Your Shepherd

Sometimes it is necessary to totally confine a puppy or an adult dog under other circumstances. Perhaps a situation arises in which a friend stops by with an unruly child who is bent on tormenting Duke. Maybe you have a visitor who is terribly allergic to dog dander, or is frightened by all dogs. Occasionally, it might be necessary to leave the doors open to the street, as when furniture is delivered or servicemen are entering and leaving the house. In those and other similar situations, crate training is extremely handy, if not essential. It is also a great help when traveling, and is preferable to a seat belt to protect and control Duke in your car.

Nuisance Behavior

Inappropriate conduct may be instinctive or learned. It might be nothing more than an extension of Duke's natural tendency to examine an object with his tongue or teeth. Great care must be taken to discourage nuisance behavior without giving him the impression that he "never does anything right."

Chewing

Mouthing or chewing is a normal side effect of being a puppy; it is said to be a dog's way of investigating or exploring his environment. Don't discourage Duke from chewing; instead, provide him with appropriate toys on which to exercise his jaw muscles. All puppies chew; the Shepherd is no worse than any other breed.

■ When possible, stop Duke *before* he gets into mischief. It's not necessary to yell at him to interrupt his adventuresome mouthing of an object. Puppies have excellent hearing and your point will be carried by a simple *"No"* if you use a gruff voice, at your usual conversational volume. When he is seen picking up an inviting object some human has left on the floor, tell him *"No"* from wherever you are; then pick up the object and put it out of his sight and reach.

■ Don't call Duke to you, then correct him. He will have forgotten what he was just doing, and will identify your scolding with his response to the *come* command. At best, this process will confuse him and prolong training time.

■ As in every other part of training, be sure he identifies your singular, crisp, stern *"No"* with his actions of the moment. It's not a good idea to repeat the *no* command several times, and it's a big mistake to stand over him, shaking your finger. Never intimidate or browbeat the pup with a correction, and don't attempt to glare him into submission. In the canine world, a prolonged stare directly into a dog's eyes is a challenge, and will accomplish nothing positive.

■ Never give Duke a worn-out shoe or an old glove to chew unless you want to put your new ski mittens at risk from that day on. You can bet he won't differentiate between your favorite jogging sneakers and his worn-out shoe. Duke will naturally be attracted to items that carry your scent and he will treasure them more than any substitute. If you can discipline yourself to keep these objects out of his reach (prevention) and give him an equally attractive object (substitution) to chew on, his manners training will proceed beautifully.

■ Provide Duke with safe, chewable dog toys. Nylon bones are fine, as are most chew sticks. Shepherd pups appreciate such toys as pressed rawhide rolls and pig ears and snout cartilage, all of which will make excellent substitutes for shoes and gloves. Another warning

will be affected by the presence of a puppy. You should be prepared to pick up your personal belongings and stow them out of reach of the pup. Children should be trained to pick up their toys and clothes at the same time you are teaching Duke to restrict his playing to his own toys.

Begging

Sitting up isn't usually thought of as a German Shepherd trick and is usually associated with smaller dog breeds. Unfortunately, it can be learned quite easily by an intelligent Shepherd youngster. It's cute when done by a puppy, but it's a nuisance when continued into adulthood. In general, begging should be ignored and discouraged from the beginning.

Shepherds are often allowed the run of the house as soon as they are housetrained. This may promote tidbit-feeding by children, which often leads to begging. The best advice in this situation is: Don't let it start. Give strict instructions that no food is allowed to pass from tiny hands to fuzzy puppies. Never allow Duke access to food scraps after meals, from the table, or any other time unless under special controlled conditions.

If Duke begins to show an interest in what's cooking in the kitchen, it's time to ban him from the room. Crate him, put him outside, or take whatever reasonable measures you must to keep him away from the kitchen when food is being prepared. Prevent him from having access to the room, and substitute his favorite chew toy for human food.

It is noted with interest that some German Shepherd owners and trainers teach

is in order: Don't give Duke a rubber squeaker toy. The small metal squeaker is easily dislodged and can cause serious problems if Duke inhales or swallows it.

- If chair legs, books, or articles on low shelves seem to interest your pup, a chemical dog repellant may be applied to them. Products such as Bitter Apple are available at pet supply stores.
- Duke may try to tug and chew on your pants leg, hand, or arm; never allow this habit to start. Instruct your children not to let him "mouth" their hands or legs. When this vice is begun, tell Duke "*No*" and substitute an acceptable toy for the hand or foot.

The potential for chewing shouldn't discourage you from obtaining a young pup, but it should alert you that your lifestyle their dogs to lie quietly in the dining room when human food is being served and eaten. This is a rather advanced training scheme, which allows them to teach their dogs that *quiet* and *down* are commands to be rewarded at the appropriate time, whereas standing up, whining, and begging result in the dog being crated or put in another room.

Pawing. Another type of nuisance begging is the act of pawing with a forefoot while the dog is sitting in front of you. This is the childlike act of a puppy, and is certainly difficult to ignore. It's flattering when Duke, of his own accord, comes to you quietly, sits down, and offers you his foot, wanting nothing more than your affection. Your first inclination is to succumb to his soulful eyes, his woebegone expression, and his obvious desire for affection. You will reach down, scratch his ears and console him with gentle words. His response will be to put both forefeet in your lap. The begging episode finally ends with Duke sitting in your lap and licking your face. It's cute when he weighs 15 or 20 pounds (6.8–9.1 kg), but cute wears thin when he weighs 80 pounds (36 kg), has just come in from a wet lawn, and you're wearing your best clothes.

The worst possible reaction to Duke's begging is to make a fuss over him, play with him, take him for a walk, or praise him. It is difficult to refrain from throwing a ten-

nis ball he has brought and placed in your lap, but if you throw it once, you will never have a moment's peace. If you respond in any fashion that can be determined to be approval of his action, you are hooked and he is in command. Bad situation!

After you have ignored him for a respectable period of time, if he has begged you to play ball, take him for a walk. If he has begged you to pet him, toss his Frisbee a few times. Just be sure he doesn't connect his begging action with your subsequent response.

Humping

It seems that every male puppy and some females exhibit this undesirable and sometimes embarrassing behavior at one time or another. You can't predict when it will happen, and no one seems to be sure *why* it happens. Often, the guilty dog has not yet reached puberty, or has been spayed or castrated, so we can't blame sexual maturation for the behavior. For whatever reason, while sitting in your living room, often with friends, Duke ambles in, singles out someone, straddles the person's leg, and begins to hump. This is the place for mild negative association training.

This errant behavior can't be tolerated, but don't lose your cool. Tell Duke *"No"* in a conversational tone. If he stops, fine; if not, pick him up or take him by the collar and move him to another room, or take him outside. He will hopefully associate his behavior with the *no* command and his isolation from your presence. Don't punish him further, and a brief period away from people should remove the incident from his mind.

The worst possible response to this behavior is to make a big issue of it. Don't let Duke think you are very upset with him; tell the friend whom he has chosen as his partner not to kick him, reprimand him, or worse still, laugh at him. Some dogs will repeat this parlor trick for the attention it receives.

Jumping Up

This bad habit usually begins when your pup is quite small, and when you have been away and return. Duke didn't mean to tear your pants or skirt; he jumped up to be nearer to your face. He didn't intend to hurt you by scratching your leg with his sharp toenails. He didn't realize his feet were muddy and you were wearing expensive hose and new shoes. Keep in mind that you taught him to come to you; that's fundamental to any dog training. Don't discourage him by getting angry, and don't sabotage your earlier training by grouching at him for running to greet you.

Instead of stepping on his toes, booting him with your knee, or yelling *"No"*

or *"Down,"* consider what you really want of this dog when he is fully grown. If you want him to bond to you, submit to your dominance, and try to please you at all times, give him credit for trying. Analyze his actions.

Why does he insist on jumping up? Because he wants to lick your face. It's a natural act of submission and greeting. A puppy's earliest memories are related to licking his mother's face to beg and hopefully receive a regurgitated meal. Puppies lick adult dogs' faces and turn belly upward as indications of submission.

Dogs of all ages want to greet friends on an equal level. Duke instinctively wants to meet you face to face. To accomplish this type of meeting, you can pick him up, but this is a problem if he just came from a muddy garden, and will be a bigger problem when he's fully grown. Better yet, you can get down to his level. Kneel when he comes running to meet you. Present your face for him to lick, and speak to him in a gentle, kind voice. Pet him, and express your love with a scratch behind the ears. When the greetings are said, stand up, tell him *"Enough"* pronouncing both syllables distinctly, and walk away.

When he becomes accustomed to your kneeling to greet him, he will probably stop jumping. If he insists on jumping up after he has been greeted, tell him *"Off,"* or *"Enough,"* and place his feet firmly on the ground. Once he retains a standing or sitting position, kneel down, give him ample praise, and walk away.

After a few such lessons he should approach you politely, and you can reach down, pet him, speak to him, scratch his ears, and move on. Never fail to reward him when he comes to you voluntarily.

If he continues to jump up, another program may help, depending on his age. This technique works best on a slightly older pup or on an incorrigible jumper. When he rambunctiously runs to you and leaps up, fall over and act hurt. It is important for you to convince him he is responsible for knocking you over. Be vocal; cry and sob. Don't speak to him, scold him, or acknowledge his presence. He will realize he isn't getting any attention, and he may begin to look sad and lick your face apologetically. When he seems to show sorrow, rise and limp away, still crying. Ignore him and his actions, and never tell him it is alright.

Don't let children tease Duke with cookies or other treats. They often hold these delicacies above their heads to keep them from the pup, and his response is to jump up on the child to reach the treat. Jumping up is not only an example of bad manners, it can cause serious problems if allowed to continue. An injured child may result from this vice.

You may also see unthinking adults who greet a dog by patting themselves on the chest, inviting the dog to jump up. Bad idea!

Barking, Crying, or Fence Running

Barking is natural when Duke senses a strange dog nearby, or when he hears unusual noises. He is expected to bark at a stranger approaching your home, especially at night. When he is hurt or ill, he

might cry and whine. These are explainable situations, but crying or barking may also be nuisance behaviors.

Barking often is a behavior the dog begins when he is bored, but continues after you have corrected the underlying problem. If you find you are spending all the time possible with your dog, and the barking persists, be sure someone isn't teasing the dog. If there is no reason for his barking, try squirting him with a high-powered squirt gun. These children's water guns can be purchased at toy stores, and are often an effective means of halting the barking vice. Of course, this corrective measure requires you to stay

59

home, and often, barking is a bad habit that persists when you are away.

Fence running is another nuisance behavior likened to the pacing often seen in caged wild animals. Often, large athletic dogs will run up and down alongside a fence continually for no apparent reason.

These behavioral vices are usually the result of loneliness or boredom. An intelligent Shepherd needs to feel he is a part of your family. When Duke begins to bark, cry, or run up and down alongside a fence for no apparent reason, you must ask yourself several questions: When was he exercised last? When did you last play ball with him, or toss a Frisbee? Has your training plan hit a snag? How long has it been since the two of you took a run in the park? Have the children been playing games with him? Have you groomed him lately? In short, have you been neglecting him? When Duke expresses boredom, are you sure you aren't the cause? Perhaps the training necessary to deal with this vice should be directed toward the other half of Duke's team.

Example: My brother's dog received more than the average amount of attention, was well mannered, had learned many toys by name, played Frisbee and fetch, and seemed to be quite well adjusted. When he was bored, however, he began running up and down the back fence, barking at birds, squirrels, or some other imaginary distraction. Neighbors complained, and something had to be done.

George rigged a garden hose nozzle aimed to squirt along the fence, directly in the dog's path. He attached a water hose to an electric pump salvaged from an old

washing machine, and wired the pump switch to a motion sensor that formerly turned on his yard lights. He aimed the motion sensor across the well-worn path, and each time his dog ran along the back fence, the sensor turned on the pump, and the dog was sprayed. I admit the rig looked rather hokey, but it certainly provided a remote negative reinforcement that stopped the dog's barking habit.

Exercise and Canine Socialization

Exercise must not be ignored at any stage of a dog's life and should be integrated into his training while he's still a pup. Although a big fenced backyard may furnish the opportunity for exercise, it does not give him the incentive. Dogs grow tired of the same yard, with the same old smells, and the same old tennis balls. They may respond to this boredom by testing the fence height or by attempting to tunnel under it.

In his early life, exercise is obtained through leash training, romping in the yard with his new human friends, and investigating all the new scents of the yard. Once he is leash trained, make use of this training to get him outside the backyard.

Meeting Other Dogs

Take Duke on daily walks, if possible. At first, it's better to confine your tours to your immediate neighborhood. After he has received some manners and rudimentary obedience training, you can more safely venture further afield. During Duke's early walks, he may meet other dogs, either through fences, on leashes, or occasionally running free.

Duke's genetic knowledge of other dogs was reinforced by his experiences while he was still in the nest. Instincts, as well as encounters with his dam and siblings, taught him the proper responses to other dogs under varying circumstances. As he grows up, each time he meets another dog he will learn more of the acceptable canine social code. As a young pup, you may see him lick the new, larger dog's face, then turn upside down. This is a natural way for a pup to display subservience to the other dog. This action tells the older dog he is not looking for trouble and wants to be friends.

Don't try to save your pup from this degrading attitude; it is a natural instinctive behavior. It's usually followed by a few moments of sniffing both ends of the puppy by the larger dog. Duke squirms and frisks about until the sniffing ritual is finished, then playfully nips at the bigger dog, pawing him, enticing him to play a game of tag.

The next time Duke encounters the same dog, he will display less of the submissive attitude, and eventually the two dogs will greet each other as acquaintances. They will exchange sniffs with familiarity and will eventually display mutual affection, or at least tolerance of one another.

Parks and Woods

As Duke matures and receives more obedience training, he can be exercised in parks and woods on his retractile leash (see page 70 for a discussion about leashes). This leash extends his freedom to investigate further afield and still gives you ultimate control over where he goes. If necessary, drive Duke to the country, the beach, or the desert for a controlled run. He will appreciate the opportunity to discover new scents and sounds, which excite and inspire him.

Body Language

These periods of exercise are fun for Duke, but to you they provide the opportunity to read his body language as he explores and scrutinizes the nooks and crannies of a newly discovered region. Pay attention to what he is telling you on his excursions. Watch his ear set, his tail movements, and his expressions. Learn what odors or scents are important to him. Talk to him as he

displays new expressions. Watch how he reacts to a fresh new animal track.

As you exercise him in the country, you will have occasion to reinforce the commands you've taught. You'll tell him *"No"* when he happens upon a dead chipmunk or starfish, or *"Come"* when he ventures a bit far, or when an approaching dog is observed. Neighbors engaged in walking, jogging, or running must be respected when they are met, with or without their dogs.

Each new incident encountered adds to Duke's understanding of his relationship with you and what you expect of him. The bond between you becomes more defined. A great variety of experiences will increase his knowledge of acceptable behavior.

Before he has received obedience training, he can be told *"Duke, say hello"* every time friends are met. This simple command lets him know everything is OK, and these people and dogs must be treated with consideration. Duke can be left standing by your side, or he can sit or lie down. Position isn't important at this stage of training. Later, after more extensive training is begun, he can be commanded *"Sit"* or *"Down"* when you wish to stop and chat with acquaintances. In both cases, he realizes he is expected to behave toward your friends with the same dignity and courtesy he displays in your home. The time you spend with your dog, teaching him and enjoying him, is rewarded by friends' comments: "What a well-mannered dog your have!"

Games People Play with Their Dogs

Your design for play should include a different object or toy for each game. A tennis ball means a game of catch, a canvas bumper or "dummy" tells Duke a fetching game is contemplated, a rubber ring is used for tug-o-war, a wooden dumbbell means a game of hide-and-seek is on the menu.

A "yard ball" made of tough nontoxic polyethylene plastic is another great toy for Duke. These balls are available in small sizes for young dogs, and 10-inch (25-cm) diameters for adult Shepherds. Duke won't be able to pick up the hollow ball, but he will devise many ways to play with it, including knocking it about with his muzzle like a soccer ball.

All toys should be kept out of Duke's reach except when they are being used. Nylon bones may be left out for him to chew at his leisure. Pressed rawhide sticks and pigs' ears will be destroyed in a short time, and should be reserved for special treats such as when he is kenneled, or must be left alone for a few hours.

Hide-and-Seek

This is a favorite game for the Shepherd pup and his family. It is best played in the house, although variations can be implemented outdoors, and is a great rainy day or evening sport. Two or more people are necessary to play this game.

1. One holds Duke very securely while the other goes into another room and hides under a bed, behind a chair, drape, or other object.
2. The holder then releases the pup, telling him "*Find* Sally." It is almost instinctive for a Shepherd to understand this game and Duke will probably follow Sally to her secret hiding place immediately. If he doesn't understand, have the hiding child softly call Duke's name once. Recognition of his name

should bring immediate results. When Sally is discovered, she can expect to have her face washed and she should respond with petting and loving.

3. After Duke has caught onto the game, increase the difficulty. The hiding child may go into a closet, but leave the door open an inch. If otherwise safe, expand the hiding places to the back-yard, garden shed, or garage. Once Duke is playing this game with prac-ticed skill, introduce more players. With a piece of clothing previously worn by the hiding child, say the child's name, let him smell the clothing, and tell Duke "*Find*." This game will teach Duke to recognize children and adults by their name and their personal scent.

If begun early and continued through-out Duke's life, this game is a very practi-cal exercise. It can be used to locate a misplaced youngster, or a friend who has wandered off.

A variation of the hide-and-seek game uses an object such as a wooden dumb-

bell, scented retrieving dummy, or some other toy reserved for the game. When you begin, name the object, show it to the dog, and let him smell it. The object is then hidden in another room and he is sent to find it. Initially, the object shouldn't be too well hidden; then, when Duke has mastered the easily found toy, it can be hidden in places more difficult to ferret out. Don't make the mistake of hiding it in a cupboard or other place Duke has been taught to avoid.

Later, you can discover Duke's tracking potential by tying a string to his scented toy, or any personal item such as a headband, wallet, or cap. It is dragged from room to room, and eventually into a hiding place. He will either seek it with his eyes, or he can use his nose to track it. When he begins to use his nose to trail the object, you can expand this game to include more interesting and difficult hiding places, and other items.

Even though this is only a game, Duke should be rewarded with appropriate adulation each time he succeeds, and he should be "helped" when he fails. Never end the game on failure. If necessary, take him to the hiding place, point, then praise him when he finds the object. Since this is an extension of his natural instincts, he need not receive food rewards when he succeeds, only your praise.

Catch

While Duke is still a puppy, one exercise he is almost sure to enjoy is a game of catch. It's a fun way to spend a few minutes or half an hour with your pal, and the game is quite simple. You toss a tennis ball to him in an arch above his head so he can easily follow it with his eyes. If he isn't able to follow it in the air, roll it across the floor to him. When he catches it, he may react in several ways. He may bring it to you to toss again, or he may decide to play chase or keep away instead, in which case you are expected to catch him and retrieve the ball. This is just a game, and there is nothing wrong with his attitude. Duke enjoys being chased, and you probably need the exercise as well.

Always use a specific toy to play catch. A tennis ball is about the right size and is soft enough that it won't hurt his mouth.

After the game is finished, put the tennis ball away. Never leave soft rubber or

foam balls lying around where they can be found and chewed.

Retrieving (Fetch)

Duke will love to play *fetch*. Some Shepherds have been used as field retrievers, although they have not gained any appreciable recognition in this discipline. Natural retrieving tendencies seem to be prevalent in the breed, often showing up before puppies are weaned. Retrieving is another game you can play as an introduction to tracking.

Fetch is a simple obedience command, a fundamental, easily understood exercise, usually connected with the dog's instinctive propensity to chase and retrieve anything moving. It is a natural for most Shepherds, but training usually depends on your dog's mental maturity.

Training can be started when Duke is very young, but if he doesn't catch on quickly, wait a week before you try again. Don't train for more than five minutes at a time, and never repeat any exercise so frequently that he loses interest in it.

Fetching Dummies

Use a small canvas dummy, or a fabric-covered lightweight object, such as a tennis ball tied in a sock. These are soft to the dog's mouth.

Duke begins this exercise by sitting next to you. Show him the dummy, throw it a dozen feet in front of you, and tell him "*Duke, fetch.*"

His first response will probably be to chase the dummy, pick it up, then wonder

what he should do with it. Give him the command "*Duke, come,*" and kneel down to his size. His name should elicit a quick run to you, but he may drop the dummy along the way. Take him back to it, ask him to "*Pick it up,*" and walk back with him to your original position. If he lacks enthusiasm in picking it up, try rubbing

NOTE: *Never toss sticks for him to catch; they might hit his eye or cause damage to his mouth. Don't throw golf balls, other hard objects that might harm his teeth, or small balls that might be swallowed. Foam balls are always dangerous to play with; they are easily chewed apart with pieces being swallowed, which might result in severe medical problems.*

a hot dog on the dummy. If he doesn't pick it up when told, hand it to him or place it in his mouth, being sure he fully understands what you expect him to do.

When he brings the dummy to you, tell him "*Give*" or "*Drop*," and take the dummy from his mouth. If he is reluctant to give it to you or to drop it, offer him a little tidbit. He can hardly accept the treat without dropping the dummy.

If Duke is slow to fetch, and runs to the dummy, then begin a game of keep-away: Attach a 30-foot (9-m) lightweight nylon check cord to his collar. Get his attention by waving the dummy closely in front of his nose. Then toss the dummy a short distance in front of him, accompanying the toss with the "*Duke, fetch*" command. When he has responded and picked up the dummy, give the *come* command as you coax him to return to you with gentle tugs on the check line. When he reaches you, tell him "*Give*" or "*Drop it*," and take the dummy from his mouth. Don't forcibly pull the dummy from his mouth; this is no time to play tug-o-war! Praise him for a job well done and repeat the exercise.

Once Duke has mastered the idea of fetching, it's time to work him without the check cord. Toss the dummy, and give him the *fetch* command. As he picks the dummy up, tell him to come. If he starts toward you immediately, stretch your hand forward to receive the dummy. If he hesitates, begin to run away from him, clapping your hands and telling him "*Come*." When he catches up to you, reach down and take the dummy from his mouth with the *give* command.

Fetching is simply a modification of his natural hunting instincts. Successes should be rewarded with praise, but usually require no treat rewards, except as needed to teach the *give* command.

It is important to make him realize the difference between the *catch* and *fetch* commands:

- *Catch* is always associated with his tennis ball. His position is across from you, facing you, where you toss the ball to him. He catches it or picks it up, and anything goes afterward.
- *Fetch* is played with a different object, usually a dummy, and he starts the game at your side. He runs to the object and returns it to you, placing it into your hand.

If you always make the distinction by using a different toy for each game, he will easily learn the difference between the commands. When you finish the *catch* or *fetch* exercise, put the ball or dummy away.

Repeat this fetching exercise daily, but not for extended periods of time. Don't allow Duke to become bored with the game. Fetching can be integrated into his other training sessions when he is taught *come*, *sit*, *stay*, and other obedience commands.

Guns

If you wish to train Duke to become accustomed to loud noises, a toy cap pistol can be used. Fire the gun at a distance from him, holding the gun behind you and pointing it away from him toward the ground. At the sound, he might be slightly startled, but you should ignore his reaction. When he sees you aren't alarmed, he will become comfortable with the noise. Never fire a gun close to his head; not only will the concussion frighten him, the noise may cause hearing impairment.

Tug-o-War

There is a difference of opinion about whether or not this game should be included in German Shepherd games. It is enjoyed by puppies and children alike, but may lead to aggressiveness in an older dog. If either you or the dog should suddenly jerk the toy, Duke's mouth or teeth may be injured. Sometimes a pup forgets where the toy ends and your hand begins. For these reasons and others, tug-o-war is probably not a good game to play with Duke.

On the other hand, if the game is supervised by an adult and the rules remain constant, it might be acceptable. Tug-o-war is always played with a specific toy, and when the game isn't being played, the toy is kept out of reach of both the pup and children.

The best object to use in tug-o-war is a hard but flexible rubber toy about 1/2 inch (1 cm) in diameter, at least a foot (30 cm) long, and shaped like a figure-eight. It should be strong enough to prevent breaking when pulled on, and tough enough so the pup can't bite it in two.

Once you decide to play tug-o-war, be sure to follow the rules.

- Don't jerk on the toy at any time.
- Don't attempt to lift Duke off his feet with the toy.

- Never slap at Duke with the rubber ring.
- Stop the activity when he gets too rambunctious or shows any signs of aggression.
- Follow this type of rough play with a cooling off period, perhaps a walk on lead.

You and your children will no doubt devise other games to play. When doing so, be sure not to let play accelerate to the stage of chewing hands, chasing and tackling children, or grabbing clothes. End any game before it becomes too rough, counterproductive, or boring.

6 Collar and Leash Training and Some Simple Tricks

Direct Negative Reinforcement

Over 100 years ago, a dog trainer made a remarkable but true statement, one that we should imprint on our minds as we embark on training. "The common belief seems to be that the dog acts from the impulse of *instinct* throughout its life. Many people concede no higher mentality to the dog than what comes from instinct, and this too notwithstanding *that true instincts are independent of experience* while the dog's *knowledge is dependent on experience and education.* A few people proceed on the theory that *punishment* will force a knowledge into the dog's consciousness." B. Waters, *Fetch and Carry*, 1895 (emphasis added).

As stated before, you should never use direct negative reinforcement when attempting to educate your dog. It is a mistake to spank or scold a mischievous pup that is guilty of nothing more than messing on the floor or picking up her leash and running with it.

Collar and Leash

Training your Shepherd to wear a collar and walk on a leash is imperative, and the earlier you start, the better. Duchess wants to follow you anyway, so all you do is add a collar, then a leash, and let her follow.

Buckle Collar

A flat buckle collar made of nylon web or leather may be purchased for Duchess at a pet supply store. Training collars made of chain or nylon should be used for most obedience training, but for elementary leash work in young puppies, a flat collar is fine. See the section on obedience training (page 84) for more information about collars.

When investing in a buckle collar for a young pup, buy one large enough to allow for growth. The flat collar should fit snugly, but not tightly; you should be able to easily slide two fingers under the collar when it is properly in place. For the first two or three days, leave the collar on Duchess only while you are with her, playing, romping, and doing the things small puppies do. After a few days of wearing her collar, she will accept and ignore it. At this point, it is safe to leave the collar on all the time.

> *Replace buckle collars every few weeks because the Shepherd puppy grows at a rapid rate. Buy a relatively cheap collar for Duchess, and check its tightness every week. When you can no longer lengthen it, buy a new one.*

The Leash

After she has become accustomed to wearing it, snap a short leash on the collar and let Duchess drag it around while she prances along behind you. Once she accepts the leash, take it in your hand and encourage her to follow you around the yard while holding the leash loosely. If she wants to chew it, tell her "*No*" in a conversational tone, and continue. In the beginning, take only a few steps at a time, coaxing Duchess to follow by extending your fingers to her. If you must, walk backwards and face your puppy to encourage her to follow.

Don't jerk or snap the lead. Although it's important to let Duchess know who has control of the leash, it should be done with gentle pressure, never roughly. Always talk to her and keep her focus on you when she is on lead. Give her praise for following you. She will soon be delighted to frolic along at your side, staying within the restrictive distances afforded by the leash. Once she makes the connection between walking on a lead

and your praise and rewards, she will welcome the appearance of her leash each day.

Pet supply stores have lightweight nylon retractile leads of various strengths and lengths. These retracting leashes are quite long and give Duchess more freedom than standard leashes. They may be used after she has become accustomed to walking on a lead, but should not be used for training.

For a week or two, work her on lead in your backyard. Once she has fully accepted the leash and its attachment to you, exercise Duchess out of the yard. The new experiences, smells, and sights are ample compensation for the restriction of the collar and leash. From this easy beginning you can gradually progress to teaching the pup to walk on your left side, in preparation for obedience training. As Duchess grows, the buckle collar should be replaced with a larger size complete with identification and vaccination tags.

Repeat some training every day if possible or at least several times a week. A puppy's attention span is very limited. In order to fix the learned behavior in her mind and make it automatic, training must be continued and repeated.

All pups are active, inquisitive, mischievous, and energetic; they sometimes misbehave. They aren't automatons; they are intelligent beings, anxious to learn and to please you. Don't make a federal case out of each mistake Duchess makes. She likes to play and have fun, and as her mentor, you should always try to make her education as painless as possible. Don't forget to play with her between exercises.

Some Simple Tricks

These tricks are best taught to puppies by using food rewards. When Duchess is more mature, she may perform for your applause, but it doesn't hurt to feed her ego with a bite of food. After all, parlor tricks are just a little beneath the dignity of a German Shepherd.

Roll Over

This trick is best taught to your pup while she is relatively small. It is a stunt willingly learned if you have earned her trust.

1. Position Duchess chest down on the lawn or carpet in front of you.
2. Place one hand between her elbows, palm upward, so you can grip her forelegs between your fingers without alarming her.

3. Take a bite of her favorite tidbit in your other hand and let her see and smell the reward. Then, with the hand holding the tidbit, extend your forefinger and circumscribe a circle in the air in front of her nose. As you do so, tell her "*Over.*"
4. With your hand resting palm up beneath her, grasp her elbows and chest and rotate her body in the same direction you have circumscribed in the air. When she has turned over and is once again chest down in front of you, give her the tidbit and plenty of praise.

Take great care not to alarm Duchess! If she is uncomfortable when you grasp her by the forelegs, relax, pet her, and begin again. Don't allow her to eat the reward until she has rotated on the floor. In other words, don't reward her for trying, only for successful completion.

If she seems frightened when you roll her over, or becomes alarmed each time you grasp her legs, reinforce her trust. Forget the tricks for a few days and hold her upside down in your arms while sitting on the floor. Scratch her tummy and rub her feet. Repeat these procedures several times a day until you can manipulate her body at will.

This, and every other trick you teach her, will progress smoothly if she trusts you. Don't betray her trust with fright or pain, or you will spoil this and future endeavors.

Repeat this exercise four or five times until she gets the feel for what you are doing. You should continue with daily repetitions until she is doing the trick smoothly every time.

Shake

This is hardly a trick, since most Shepherds will come to their owners several times a day and extend the hand of friendship. In case Duchess hasn't already started it, you can teach her this in an afternoon. Remember that dogs associate your word command with an action, and the command might be any sound, one you can invent for the occasion. *Shake* is the traditional command; *gimme five* or a similar command might suit your purpose better. Just be sure you use the same command every time.

1. Begin training while sitting in a chair. Call Duchess to you and have her sit on the floor facing you. This is easily done by giving her the *sit* command or pushing her bottom to the floor.
2. While you both are sitting, facing each other, extend your right hand toward her while holding a little tidbit in your left hand slightly above the level of her eyes, where it can easily be seen. The sight of this tasty morsel immedi-

ately in front of her face will encourage her to sit and remain in a sitting position.

3. Give the command you have selected, "*Shake*," or something similar. Immediately pick up her right foot in your right hand, praise her with a "*Good dog*," and give her the tidbit.
4. Hold her paw for a second, then let it drop.
5. Repeat this several times then go outside and play catch or take her for a walk. Later in the day, call her to you and repeat the drill.

Shaking hands has several variations you might wish to use instead of the traditional *shake*. You can teach her to first offer her left paw, for which you give her no reward but tell her, "*That's your left paw. Ladies shake with their right hand. Give me your right paw.*" Then when she offers her right paw, she gets the treat.

Sound Off

This trick can become a nuisance, and one Duchess might use to get attention or snacks; however, it has another more useful purpose. If a dog will sound off or bark on verbal command, she can be taught to do so every time the phone or doorbell rings, or when she smells smoke.

The best way to teach Duchess to sound off is to discover something that always causes her to bark, perhaps the doorbell or a knock at the door. You can encourage her barking by calling her attention to the knocking and making an issue of it. *"What's that, Duchess? Who's there, girl?"*

Some dogs will quietly woof when they see another dog outside the window, or when the mailman approaches the porch. Any such event can be used if it routinely stimulates a sound from Duchess, no matter how faint her bark is in the beginning.

Once you have found something in her life that always stimulates a bark, even a tiny one, you have the key. Let's say every time someone knocks at the door, Duchess quietly woofs. You simply use the knock to condition her to bark on command.

1. Have a friend come to the door at a specified moment. Be ready with a tidbit hidden in your pocket.
2. While both you and Duchess are sitting in the room, your friend knocks loudly on the door. You quickly tell Duchess *"Sound off,"* she barks, you say *"Good dog,"* and you reinforce the praise with a tidbit.
3. The friend goes away, but returns later at a prearranged time to repeat the performance. When the sudden, loud knock comes, immediately give Duchess the verbal *sound off* command. When she barks, praise her and give her the reward. In no time, Duchess will sound off on your command, whether or not a knock is heard.

If you decide to teach Duchess to sound off, another useful command to teach is *quiet*. It is best taught as you are teaching *sound off*, and will give you some control over nuisance barking habits under various circumstances. Reinforcing the *quiet* command with a pat on the head and a *"Good dog"* should impress upon her that she has done nothing wrong when she barks, but it's now time to cease and desist.

Settle or Pick a Spot

This quick trick is one that will be appreciated for the life of your dog. Very early in Duchess's life, you will find there are certain times when she is underfoot and would be more appreciated if she would just camp somewhere.

Teaching her this trick requires nothing more than giving her the command you have selected (*"Settle"*) and leading her to the blanket or bed you have provided and placed in the same room you are in. Once there, she should be taught to lie down, using her nylon bone or chew stick as a reward. Once she is settled, you should praise her and pet her and take your chair once again. When she begins to rise from her spot, tell her *"No"* in a gruff voice. When she settles again, praise her.

7 Canine Good Citizen Certificate

What Is a Canine Good Citizen?

As the title implies, the holder of this certificate is well mannered and trained to act with decorum and obedience. A canine good citizen shares his owner's activities with predictably good behavior. He is a dog that can be taken for a walk without pulling and tugging at his leash, a dog that doesn't embarrass his owner on each corner by threatening every dog in sight.

He is a dog that, when left loose in the house as guests arrive, will greet them courteously and respectfully without causing commotion, jumping up, or growling. A canine good citizen displays acceptable behavior at all times and is a pleasure to be around. In other words, Duke is a valuable pet, not a nuisance problem.

Good citizen training doesn't take the place of lessons in manners, obedience training, or any other type of instruction. For some companion dogs, good citizen training is the end product. It's where you want your dog to be and is quite sufficient in and of itself.

On the other hand, this training can form a beginning for obedience training, tracking, searching, or other disciplines. It is a step above good manners and leash training, but should be viewed in the same light. Passing a test that is given by a local AKC dog club will earn Duke a certificate that will tell the world you care enough for your dog to spend the time to train him properly.

Technique

The first training axiom is the same as before. Treat successes with positive reinforcement, show no reaction to failures, and don't bore the dog.

You can't reason with your Shepherd in any training program, regardless of how informal it is. Give Duke a command, and insist he obeys. Be careful not to reward half-successes or almost-accomplishments. Don't nag. It shouldn't be necessary to repeat commands endlessly. Teach him what each command means, and how to respond to those commands. Exert yourself as the boss, but do so without verbal or physical abuse.

If there is a key to good citizen training, it is to gain your Shepherd's confidence and direct his concentration on *you* and what you are doing. As soon as he has shown a propensity to watch you at all times, anticipating your commands and focusing his attention on your voice and hands, he is ready to begin training.

Good Citizen Certificate

The Canine Good Citizen (CGC) test was accepted by the American Kennel Club in 1989 and since then has grown steadily in popularity. Parts of the test are presently in use by the Delta Society and Therapy Dogs International. It is the only event sponsored or sanctioned by the AKC that includes mixed-breed dogs. It consists of an examination by an experienced evaluator to determine a dog's public behavior. This examination is not competitive; dogs are tested alone. Following AKC guidelines, dog clubs throughout the United States administer the test. Dogs that pass the test receive a certificate from the AKC.

Dogs are evaluated in ten different exercises, all of which help to assure that the dogs are good neighbors. There are no points involved; the scoring is a simple pass or fail evaluation. The dogs are evaluated on essential, easily taught activities, which include the following exercises.

1. Accepting a Friendly Stranger. This exercise demonstrates your control of Duke when a friendly person is met on the street or in your home. He is expected to allow the person to approach without displaying any aggression or resentment such as barking or growling.

In testing, the evaluator walks up to you and Duke, stops, talks, and shakes hands with you, while ignoring Duke. Duke passes this test if he shows no signs of aggression or timidity, but keeps his position without going to either you or the evaluator.

Training in this case is quite simple. It only requires Duke to be comfortable with strangers, which means you must exercise him in public places. You can teach him to sit or stand quietly by using positive control of his leash.

To train, you need the help of several people with whom your dog is not familiar. When your friendly stranger approaches, tell Duke to sit, then quietly step on his leash, holding him in place. Your helper greets you, shakes your hand, and converses with you for a few seconds, then he moves on, and Duke is rewarded if he has remained calmly in place.

If this training is begun while he is a pup, Duke will never be shy of friends you meet on the street. If you are consistent in controlling him in place, he will never try to bounce around or jump up on your friends.

2. Sitting Politely for Petting. This test is nothing more than demonstrating the tenets of a well-mannered dog. You will have Duke sit on either side of you. You may use a *sit-stay* command if he has mastered that phase of obedience training. If not, refer to the obedience section of this book (pages 89–93) and review the training method described.

Once Duke is in the sitting position, the evaluator will approach and pet him on his head and body, then circle you and your dog. During the evaluator's handling, you can talk to Duke, assuring him of your approval. To pass the test, Duke must not show shyness or aggressiveness. He must passively allow petting in the manner described when you have put him in the sitting position.

Once again, it is important to keep Duke's concentration on you, rather than on the evaluator. If he is looking at you, watching your hands, listening to your voice, he will have no trouble with this exercise. This is yet another example of the ease of training your Shepherd while he is young. When teaching an adult dog, training time will be multiplied.

3. Appearance and Grooming. The evaluator will approach and inspect Duke to determine if he is clean, well groomed, and has a healthy weight and appearance. The evaluator then lightly brushes or combs your dog, inspecting his ears and picking up each foot in turn. Duke is allowed to sit or stand during this exercise, and you are expected to verbally assure him at all times.

This exercise is also best taught when Duke is young. From the time you acquire him, ask your family members, dog-owning friends, and interested parties to participate. A well-mannered dog should be amenable to grooming by anyone when you are present.

4. Out for a Walk. This is another control exercise. Unlike *heeling* in obedience training, Duke may be on either side, but you must have him under leash control. In the test, you will be given specific directions by the evaluator. You must turn left,

right, reverse your direction, and stop, as instructed. You are allowed, even encouraged, to talk to Duke as you proceed through this exercise.

This task is likewise taught to a puppy at a very young age and is often a forerunner to the obedience exercise known as *heeling*. The differences are that the leash is kept loose, the dog needn't be in the AKC *heel* position, and he isn't required to sit when you stop, nor walk on your left. (You will find other exercises in this test more easily accomplished if

you always keep Duke on your left.) The instructions for this exercise are covered in the section on obedience training (see page 92), and won't be repeated here.

5. Walking Through a Crowd. This simple exercise is easily taught to Duke as soon as he is leash trained. It requires no more from him than walking on leash in a public place. The evaluator asks you to take him alongside at least three people, some of whom are accompanied by their dogs.

To pass the test, he can show natural interest, but no aggressiveness or shyness, and he shouldn't demonstrate lack of

control by tugging at the leash, barking, or trying to play. You may talk to Duke and encourage him during the exercise. Be sure to praise him when the two of you have passed the examination.

Training for this phase of the test is about what you would expect. Walk him on quiet streets of town, keeping him under control by means of your voice and the leash. Progress to busier streets as time passes. You can employ the assistance of several neighborhood friends. Have them stand around, perhaps with a well-behaved dog on a leash as you take Duke on lead through this small crowd. If necessary, bait him with a treat when he shows interest in others. Keep his interest focused on you by talking to him continuously.

6. *Sit* and *Down* on Command/Staying in Place. This is an owner-control test with several parts. The first part of the test entails giving Duke the *sit*, followed by the *down* command.

These commands are followed by the second part of the test, which is the *stay* command. Duke is tested while wearing a 20-foot (6.1-m) leash—which never leaves your hand—and measures your influence on your dog while you walk away from him and return to his side.

The test is begun when you are instructed to put your dog in the *down* or *sit* position and tell him "*Stay*." Gentle guidance may be used to encourage him to take the position, but most evaluators prefer that you don't touch your dog. You may not force Duke or use food to cause him to assume the desired position. The evaluator then tells you to leave your dog. You walk the length of the 20-foot line and Duke must stay in place, but may change positions. You are then instructed to return to your dog, take your former position beside him, and release him from the *stay*.

Staying is discussed fully in the section on obedience training (page 90). It differs from obedience commands in that you are allowed to encourage and guide Duke into either of the two positions, and you maintain control through the long check line.

7. Coming when Called. This good citizen task displays the dog's obedience in coming to his owner when called. First tell Duke to stay or wait, then leave him and walk 10 feet (3 m) away. Turn and face Duke and call him. You may use encouragement such as patting your leg or motioning with your hands. The evaluator, meanwhile, may mildly distract Duke by petting him. Training for this exercise is covered in the manners discussion on page 48.

8. Reaction to Another Dog. This exercise is a bit more difficult for puppies and is a real test of their ability to concentrate. With Duke on lead, you walk across the floor, or down the sidewalk. You meet a stranger who also has a polite, well-behaved dog on a leash. When you meet, you stop, exchange pleasantries, shake hands, and continue your stroll for another 5 yards (4.6 m). Duke may show casual interest in the other dog, but must remain in your control. Dogs generally pass on the outside of their handlers, and usually the dog sits when you stop, but sitting is not mandatory. If you have

trained Duke to walk on your left, and the dog being met is on his handler's left, the exercise is much smoother.

This training is similar to other exercises. Get and keep Duke's focus. Obtain the help of several friends with well-behaved dogs. Ask them to take their dogs, on leash, up and down the sidewalk or across the yard. They should keep their dogs on their left side while walking. As you approach your friend, gently tighten Duke's leash a bit, signaling him of your awareness of the oncoming dog. This will shift his concentration from the dog to you. Talk to him and keep his focus on you. Steady him as he walks on your left side. Leash control is very important in this exercise, and a training collar should be used (see page 84 for discussion of training collars).

In the first phase of training, follow the foregoing directions and pass the friend and dog without stopping. Keep Duke's lead snug, controlling his actions. Speak to your friend, who will return the greeting and, after passing them, reward Duke according to his performance. If he only looked over his shoulder at the passing dog, he has made a good start and deserves a perfunctory reward. If he tugged at the lead, give him no reward. If he watched you, listening for commands, and hardly looked at either the person or dog, he should receive praise and perhaps a tidbit.

Repeat this training until Duke passes dogs with no second thought, then introduce the second phase, which is to stop and talk for a few seconds with the person, shake hands, and continue your walk. When you stop, it is an excellent idea (but

not mandatory) to put Duke in a *sit-stay* position.

9. Reacting to Distractions. This exercise tests Duke's confidence. The evaluator has several distractions from which to choose. Usually, he selects a sound distraction such as the slamming or sudden opening of a door. Another sound commonly used is dropping a book flat on the floor 10 or 12 feet (3–3.5 m) behind Duke. The evaluator also may knock over a chair 6 or 8 feet (2–3 m) from Duke or ask you to pass people who are engaged in loud

talk and backslapping about 10 feet (3 m) from Duke.

Another part of the test is a visual distraction. It may be a person on a bicycle who rides about 6 feet (2 m) from your dog, or someone pushing a rattling grocery cart passing about 10 feet (3 m) from Duke. The distraction might be a person running across your path or a person crossing your path on crutches, in a wheelchair, or using a walker.

In order to pass this test, Duke may watch these happenings with natural curiosity, but he shouldn't panic, try to escape from them, bark, or show any aggressiveness or fear.

Training consists of repeated exposure to these types of distractions. You can stage the sound distractions with the help of a friend. While exposing Duke to various sounds, include whistles and horns with those previously mentioned. By your voice and tone, let Duke know he is safe. Control his actions with the lead. The sounds warrant his attention but should not be feared. Keep his focus on you at all times.

Visual distractions are best handled by walking Duke on streets where cars, bikes, skateboards, and motor scooters are buzzing around. Keep him a significant distance from these distractions at first, then gradually change your path to bring Duke closer. Never put yourself or your dog in danger. Later, when you feel Duke has excellent concentration on your voice and his leash, you might try walking through a supermarket parking lot. If you can safely walk in a lot where grocery carts are pushed back and forth, do so, but remember parking lots are dangerous places during busy hours.

Keep a steady conversation going with Duke while these distractions take place around him. Tell him *"Take it easy,"* signal him through his lead, letting him know he should stay at your side and not panic.

10. Supervised Separation. This exercise tests the ability of your dog to be left alone for three minutes without panicking or showing excessive agitation. It is accomplished by having Duke on a 6-foot (1.8-m) lead. Hand the lead to an appointed evaluator and leave Duke's field of vision for three minutes.

Until Duke has earned his CGC certification and has also been certified by one of the therapy organizations, he should not be taken into a nursing or assisted living center, even if invited by the management.

Duke will pass the test if he remains with the evaluator without chewing or tugging the lead, barking, pacing, or whining. He doesn't need to sit or lie down, and may move about, providing he remains calm and quiet and doesn't pull at his leash. He may be interested in where you go, display mild agitation or nervousness, and be eager for your return.

Training for this exercise is easier if Duke has been taught the *wait* command, as discussed under Crate Training (page 53).

Occasionally tie him for short periods of time while you walk around the house and out of sight. Each time, tell him *"Wait"* and gradually increase the time you are away. It is very important for you to reward him with praise when he waits patiently for you. This task can be practiced in front of your home, in your backyard, or in any safe public place.

AKC member clubs make CGC evaluations, and information about them may be obtained by contacting the AKC or an all-breed club in your community. Having a Canine Good Citizen Certificate hanging on the wall is evidence that Duke has been trained. It means you love him enough to spend the time training him, and Duke has become a good neighbor.

8 *Obedience Training*

Overview

Obedience trials are competitions for all AKC-registered dogs. In an Obedience trial, Duchess may be entered into competition with dozens of dogs of many different breeds. Formal Obedience work begins with the Novice level, progresses through the Companion Dog level, and finally to the Companion Dog Excellent and Utility levels. These various stages of Obedience training may lead to other, rather specialized training such as Schutzhund, Tracking, and search and rescue. However, such specialized training isn't a continuation or more advanced type of Obedience work. Tracking, as encountered in Obedience Utility Dog training, may be continued to produce a Tracking Dog, but the specially trained tracker can perform quite nicely with minimal Obedience work and no Obedience titles.

If you are serious about training an Obedience dog to compete in trials, contact your local German Shepherd Dog club and enroll your dog and yourself in formal training classes. This hands-on training is irrefutably the best for you and your dog. Class participation will help you set goals and standards, and will measure your progress as well as that of your dog.

In an obedience class you will work with other people who have common interests, and the other dogs in the class are an integral part of obedience training. It is virtually impossible to completely prepare your dog for Obedience trials at home in the absence of other trainers and dogs.

Early obedience training can be staged in your yard, but as soon as practical, you should choose another place for Duchess' schooling. Dog club classes are usually held in convenient and neutral places nearby.

That said, it is practical to teach your dog some commands before you progress to class work. You and your Shepherd can accomplish a great deal at home. Obedience classes usually won't take pups until they are four or even six months old. You can be well ahead of the class if you start when Duchess is a young pup.

Obedience training is a stepwise endeavor that is best taught in short sessions of a few minutes each. As in any other training, the dog will remember more from short practice periods than from longer ones. Younger dogs need shorter lessons than older animals. You should always watch Duchess' attention span, and when she shows any sign of boredom, stop the lesson. An entire training session shouldn't continue any longer than 5 to 15 minutes, and the individual lesson shouldn't be repeated more than three to five times. You can, however, repeat the training session several times a day.

Purpose of Obedience Trials

Formal Obedience trials are designed to demonstrate the usefulness of purebred dogs in companion relationships with humans. They measure a dog's ability to perform certain tasks according to set rules. Each participant in a class performs the same exercises in the same way and is scored by the same judge. The primary objective of each phase of an Obedience trial is to demonstrate the training and conditioning of a dog in every conceivable circumstance. Trials promote and display

exemplary dog behavior in all situations, in public places, and in the presence of strange dogs and their handlers.

An obedience trial measures a dog's willingness and enjoyment of the work as well as the ability to perform according to somewhat arbitrary standards. Dogs competing in Obedience trials must be properly trained, but to score well, they must also show smartness and class in performing the many tasks of the trial. Good Obedience dogs are practiced and smooth, but the judges also look for happy dogs, not dull, disinterested robots.

Equipment

Training equipment is much like various suits of clothes; each piece of equipment means something different when placed on the dog. Duchess will soon understand what to expect by the equipment she is fitted with.

Training (Choke) Collar

A piece of equipment commonly referred to as a choke collar should be used for obedience training. "Choke collar" is a misnomer if the collar is used correctly. It is formed from a short length of smooth chain, a flat nylon tape, or strong nylon cord with a ring fastened to each end. The ring through which the chain is dropped to form a noose is called the dead ring. The ring on the opposite end, into which the leash is fastened, is called the training ring.

In order to work as designed, the training collar must be properly fitted to the dog. One size won't fit Duchess from puppyhood to adulthood. It should measure approximately 2 inches (5.1 cm) greater than the circumference of her neck. Most Shepherds respond equally well to either nylon or chain training collars.

To form the collar, drop the chain (or cord) through one of the rings, then attach the lead snap to the training ring. Place the collar on the dog so that the end of the collar attached to the leash comes up the dog's left side and crosses from left to right over the top of her neck. Duchess is maintained on your left side, and when it is necessary to correct the dog's action, the collar is given a gentle tug, then released. If a training collar is placed on the dog's neck incorrectly, it will not release quickly, and may injure the dog. A training collar that is too long will not close quickly enough to be effective. Keep in mind that the dog will be walking on your left side at all times.

Pronged Collars

Training collars of a more severe type are available. They are constructed of a dozen or so hinged wire prongs. The dull prongs turn against the dog's neck when the leash is tightened. They may be an effective way of training an obstreperous dog, but rarely if ever are they needed on a biddable Shepherd. They should be used only by professional trainers (if necessary), and when used, must never be abused. Prong collars are banned from the premises of all AKC shows.

Leash

For training, a short, lightweight, leash is best. Use a 4-foot (120-cm) web or leather lead to allow control of Duchess's actions. A lead shouldn't coil up in your hand or hang down to distract the dog.

Formal Obedience Trial Training

As discussed at the beginning of this chapter, preparation for Obedience competition should be accomplished by participation in a class with an instructor. Obedience rules, or their interpretation, are often changed. It is impossible to simulate the presence of other people and dogs while working with Duchess alone. Regardless of how well she responds to your basic commands at home, she will be distracted by new faces and smells in the competition ring. Recall commands, working off lead, and hand signals are all best taught in classes.

To prepare you and your dog for a trial, join an obedience club or participate in classes sponsored by your breed club or an all-breed club. Equipment such as bar jumps, hurdles, and other props, which are specialized parts of obedience training, are usually owned by a club and furnished for training of their members' dogs.

Obedience Club Classes

- Monitor the class before you join.
- Check the instructor's attitude and knowledge and both the human and canine students, and, if you aren't favorably impressed, look for another class.
- Don't get involved with classes that insist on long, trying lessons, or lessons that *must* be taught every day. Such adventures usually end in dreary, drudging performances and eventual burnout.
- Make a commitment to attend the class you join. They reserve space for you and you have an obligation to be there with your dog if you sign up. Don't waste their time and yours with a half-hearted attempt. If you aren't serious, don't sign up, but if you sign up, abide by the instructor's rules. You must do your homework if you and your dog are to succeed. The instructor isn't going to train Duchess for you. If you disagree with methods being taught, resign.
- Don't make the class wait for you; be prompt.
- The class must advance at the pace of the slowest dog or the slowest human in the class, and the results may fall short of your expectation. Don't be discouraged.

The first lesson is usually for handlers without their dogs. Use this time to get everything clear in your mind about your obligations as well as the methods being used.

Sanctioned Matches

These are learning tools. They are informal Obedience trials held by clubs to meet the "finishing" needs of young dogs, dogs recently trained, and handlers who have never been in a formal Obedience trial. They invoke all the rules of an AKC trial and usually award ribbons to winners. Winners in sanctioned matches do not receive credits toward Obedience titles.

Fun Matches

These are Obedience functions held according to some of the rules of an AKC Obedience trial. They are just what the name implies—fun to participate in and fun to observe. Clubs often sponsor these fun matches to get people interested in Obedience. They are not held under the AKC rules, and obviously, no credits are accumulated toward Obedience titles.

Classes, Exercises, and Awards

Novice A obedience classes and Novice B classes are for dogs six months or older that haven't earned a Companion Dog (CD) title. Novice exercises *consist of heel on leash and figure eight, stand for examination, heel free, recall, long sit*, and *long down*.

The AKC awards a CD title to a dog that has received qualifying scores at three licensed or member Obedience trials, under three different judges, providing that at least six dogs were competing in each trial.

Open A Class is for dogs that have won the CD title but haven't won a Companion Dog Excellent (CDX) title. The dog's owner or a member of her family must handle the dog.

Open B Class is for dogs that have won the CD title or a CDX title or a Utility Dog (UD) title. The owner or any other person may handle these dogs.

The exercises for open classes consist of *heel free and figure eight, drop on recall, retrieve on flat, retrieve over high jump, broad jump, long sit*, and *long down*.

A CDX title may be awarded by the AKC to a dog that has received qualifying

scores at three Obedience trials judged by three different judges.

Utility A Class is for dogs that have won the CDX title but not the UD title. The dog's owner or a member of his immediate family must handle the dog.

Utility B Class is for dogs that have won the CDX or UD title; any person may handle them.

Utility exercises involve a *signal exercise, scent discrimination article 1, scent discrimination article 2, directed retrieve, moving stand and examination*, and *directed jumping*.

A UD title is awarded to a dog that has received qualifying scores by three different judges in three Obedience trials. Forty-seven German Shepherd Dogs earned UD titles in 1997.

Utility dogs may earn points toward the coveted Obedience Trial Championship (OTCh). These points are awarded for each first or second place ribbon won in UD classes, according to the number of dogs competing. A dog must accumulate no less than 100 points under specific circumstances. Two German Shepherd Dogs earned OTCh titles in 1997.

Utility Dog Excellent (UDX) is a title awarded to dogs that have earned, at ten separate events, qualifying scores in both the Open B and Utility B classes. There are other specific rules applying to these wins. The UDX title is used after the dog's name when the title has been earned. Eight German Shepherd Dogs earned UDX titles in 1997 competitions.

Home Schooling

In this chapter many training procedures are discussed that you can use in your home and in the backyard. All such exercises are good for the dog and the teacher, but in order to be of significant value, they must be repeated time and again in more public places. *Heel* may work fine in your backyard, but the command shouldn't be trusted until it is proven on the street.

Elementary Training

Shepherds are naturals for obedience training, but don't be discouraged when Duchess occasionally becomes obstinate, sits down, drags her feet, or refuses to listen or cooperate. Don't lose your cool! Have patience and take your time; this is a new business to her and what isn't learned today will come naturally tomorrow. As in all training, never end a session with a failure. If your pupil doesn't cooperate, shift to another task, one she has already learned, reward her amply, and stop training for the day.

Leads and collars tell the dog what your intentions are.

- The training collar, whether chain or fabric, tells Duchess you intend to maintain maximum control. She will expect obedience work or show training.
- The everyday web collar is worn at all other times, except when she is in tracking training.
- The web collar and short leash tell her this is to be an exercise time or a controlled walk.

- The web collar and long retracting lead, or no lead at all, mean a romp in the dog park.

Hopefully, when you begin, the pup will have already accepted her leash. Remove the web or leather collar and put a training (choke) collar in its place, snap on the sturdy nylon web leash, and you are ready to begin the first lesson.

Command Clarity

Complex, multiword commands are difficult for a puppy to comprehend. Commands should contain as few words as possible. Say them distinctly and rather curtly or crisply, in a different tone than you use in typical conversation. Each command should be separated into several parts.

Giving commands in the German language is ridiculous and unnecessary. German has no special meaning for American-born Duchess. Your own language will work just as well, and your native tongue is probably English. You do not need to teach commands that are identical to those taught by other trainers.

However, it is very important for each command to be associated with a word or sound unlike any other that may be used in Duchess's training. Think about how a command sounds to Duchess. Be sure one command doesn't rhyme with another, or with your dog's name. Find the specific single word you wish to associate with a task, then stick with it.

Shouting isn't going to add anything positive to her training; Duchess has better hearing than you. Neither should the command be repeated time and again for a single function. The tone in which a command is given is as important as the command. Use a special voice modulation for commands. You aren't asking her to *please* perform a certain exercise, you are *telling* her to do so. Your voice tone for a command must be altogether different from your verbal praise given when she performs correctly. Practice giving commands in the pup's absence, then practice softening your voice for praise. Your particular words of praise aren't as important as the manner and tone in which they are delivered.

When giving a command, first, say the dog's name clearly. This is difficult when her name is complex or lengthy, so if necessary, shorten the name and make it simple. Use a one- or two-syllable name; if you have named your dog Chrysanthemum, shorten it to Chrys. It is possible Duchess's name will be shortened to Dutch, when you begin training.

Sit

To teach Duchess to sit, follow these steps:

1. Stand Duchess with her rump to a wall.
2. Say *"Duchess."* That will call her to attention; wait a second or two.
3. Say *"Sit."* That tells her what you want her to do.
4. Enforce the command by offering her a tidbit that you hold slightly above her muzzle and in front of her eyes. Slowly move the tidbit toward her rear. She will back up a step, feel the wall, and sit. If you do not want to use a food treat, cradle her muzzle in your hand and tilt her nose upward. this alternate method usually works as well.

> **NOTE:** *Acceptable methods of training change with the times. A few years ago, pushing a dog's bottom to the floor, accompanied by a subsequent reward, was a time-honored method of teaching a dog to sit. This worked fine when the dog was a quick study and anxious to please, but this method has given way to other techniques in recent times.*

5. Once she is sitting, reward with praise, petting, and perhaps a food treat.
6. Say *"OK"* to release her from the exercise.

That same technique is used for most simple commands and eliminates forcing

her rump to the ground. When she recognizes the command and reacts on key, she will perform appropriately anywhere she happens to be. For instance, if you are taking her on a walk and you want to stop for a minute to talk to your neighbor, use the following technique.

1. With your puppy at your left side, in a calm, normal voice, say "*Duchess.*" Pause a second, then say "*Sit.*"
2. When the command has been absorbed, cause the pup's bottom to sink to the ground. Never use the term "*Sit down,*" because *sit* is one task and *down* is another. To let the dog understand exactly what you desire, it's important to allow a few seconds after the *sit* command is given before you proceed. Duchess must always associate the command with the desired action.
3. After your *sit* command, offer her a small tidbit slightly above eye level, immediately in front of and very close to her muzzle. This will encourage her to back up slightly and sit.
4. When she sits, give her the morsel and after a few seconds of sitting, release her by saying, "*OK,*" then praise her.

A tidbit reward is sometimes used in the beginning of any training, but praise must be given in abundance after the correct performance of each exercise. When the pup doesn't perform the exercise correctly, don't make a big issue about her error. Say "*Wrong*" in a crisp, conversational tone, before you make the correction. Reserve the word "*No,*" given in a gruff voice, for times when Duchess is in trouble and you want her to cease the mischief in which she is involved.

Practice the sitting exercise several times a day, but don't expect miracles—if you're lucky, the dog will catch on the first day, but don't count on it. Don't add to her confusion with more training at this time.

In the next session, practice the *sit* command several times, and if you meet with success, progress to another exercise. If it takes several daily sessions to learn to sit correctly, so be it; you're in no hurry, and some dogs take longer than others to catch on. Ten-week-old puppies have short attention spans, and aren't usually as quick to learn simple exercises as older dogs are.

Stay

When Duchess has mastered sitting, and is waiting for her praise, tell her "*Stay,*" while you remain standing at her right side.

1. Present your flat outstretched palm in front of her muzzle as you give the *stay* command. If she tries to lie down or stand up, tell her "*Wrong,*" put her back in the *sit* position, and repeat the command "*Stay.*"
2. After a few seconds, release her from the *stay* with an "*OK,*" and give her a reward. Again, the command is broken into several parts; first, the dog's name, then the command, then the action, the release, and finally, the reward.
3. The next step is to move away from Duchess while she is obeying the *stay* command. When you put the leash on the ground and start to walk away, the faithful pup will try to follow. In a conversational tone, say "*Wrong,*" place

Duchess in the sitting position, repeat the *stay* command, display your outstretched flat palm, and back away again. After a few tries, she will get the idea and stay put while you take several steps backward; then you must return to her side to finish the exercise.

4. Don't forget to release her from the *stay*, and never finish the exercise without reward.

One word of caution: Don't expect too much of a puppy. Take only a few steps away in the beginning. Don't push Duchess to the limit and expect her to stay interminably like the well-trained dogs you have seen in obedience trials. Return quickly to her side, take your position with your dog on your left, pick up the leash, and release her from the *stay* command.

In the beginning, most pups are doing well if they stay for 20 seconds without fidgeting. Remember that you can't reward her unless she does the task correctly. When you extend the *stay* for a longer time than she is ready for, you risk being unable to reward her. It is important for her to always think she is right, and always receive a reward.

Down

This is another topic undergoing change among American dog trainers. Methods that were in vogue in the past are rapidly becoming passé. Contemporary trainers often don't force dogs to the ground with their hands, nor do they lift them or touch them to cause a desired response. The currently acceptable method uses food or lures to cause proper response. Only you, the trainer, can try the various techniques and decide which works best for Duchess and you.

The *down* command is used in Obedience trials, and is also a convenient way to let the pup relax while you talk to neighbors on your daily walks. This is also one of the few obedience commands used in tracking.

1. Begin the exercise with the dog in the sitting or standing position. Be sure to hesitate between the dog's name and the command. "*Duchess* (hesitation), *down*" is the command. Don't muddy the issue with extra words. Never tell the dog "*Lie down.*"
2. After you have given the *down* command, cause her body to reach the ground, slowly and gently. Don't fight her. When necessary to encourage her to lie down, hold a tidbit so low and close to her muzzle that she can't reach it without lying down. It's sometimes best to begin the exercise with Duchess

leaving her, and if she stays you will return with more praise and perhaps a tidbit, she will be happy to cooperate.

Stand

This exercise will be invaluable as you progress to actual judged shows and trials. Teaching Duchess to stand can be done either of two ways. The simplest is to give the command, "*Duchess, stand*," followed by levering her into a standing position with your right arm. If you wish to teach her without force, there is another method.

1. Stand her over a small, smooth board 2 inches by 4 inches (5 cm × 10 cm), laid on edge on the ground, and give her the *stand* command. Sitting or lying on this board will be uncomfortable, and she will undoubtedly stand.
2. Be sure to release her with your "*OK*," and praise her after she has stood for a minute without moving.

in a sitting position and fold her elbows, placing her belly against the ground.

Another trick to use when training the *down* command is to work with Duchess on a low table. Give the command "*Duchess* (hesitation), *down*." As soon as "*Down*" is spoken, hold a morsel in front of her, below the level of her feet. She will probably lie down quickly of her own accord, and you can reward her with the tidbit. Take care never to allow Duchess to fall or jump from the table.

3. After the *down* command is accepted and performed routinely on command, you can progress to the next command.
4. *Stay* is again accompanied by backing away a few steps while she is in the *down* position. Finish the exercise by returning to her, releasing her from the exercise, and lavishing great praise upon her. Once the pup realizes you aren't

Heel

Heeling is an obedience exercise that all well-behaved dogs should learn. But, before you begin, you must realize that what you ask of Duchess is contrary to her instinctive nature and she must follow the pure, arbitrary rules you have devised. She must walk on your left side with her nose in a certain position and she must anticipate your changes of speed and your stops.

With what instinctive behavior can this exercise be compared? Absolutely none. It is ridiculous to try to instill this behavior into a dog's mind, yet thousands of dogs are taught to heel each year.

1. Position Duchess on your left side, running the leash through your left hand, holding it with your right.
2. Give her the command, *"Duchess, sit."* Hesitate a moment, then, as you step off with your right foot, give the command, *"Heel."* In Obedience trials, the *heel* position has the dog's neck centered on your left hip. This is accomplished by applying gentle pressure on her training collar, and when she is in the proper position, releasing the pressure.
3. If she continually wants to lag behind, you can encourage her to keep up by baiting her with a tidbit held in your right hand.

Soon, Duchess will be walking by your side, taking turns and stops in her stride. Remember, these instructions are not designed to ready you and Duchess for Obedience trial competition. These lessons are for home schooling, and will get you both started.

Heeling is a tough exercise for an ambitious puppy to master. Duchess is often anxious to forge ahead and investigate something at the far end of her leash. Keep the leash short, but don't hold it too tightly. At first, leave enough slack for her to move a step ahead or behind you, but don't allow her to bolt ahead. If she continually moves past your left knee, do an about-face, and walk in the opposite direction. Say *"Duchess, heel"* as you make the turn. Soon, Duchess will watch where you put your left foot and keep her body in line with you. Above all, talk to your heeling dog. Let her know she is doing what you want, tell her *"Atta girl"* when she is walking in the proper position. If you have had to correct her by tightening her leash, let her know she is doing well now.

After she has properly heeled for a dozen steps, stop, and push her bottom to the ground to the sitting position as you give the *sit* command. Then release her with an *"OK,"* reward her with praise if she has performed satisfactorily, and repeat the exercise once or twice.

Heeling is a necessary part of obedience training and is often used when going to and from the ring in dog shows. It is great when you need to exert maximum control of your dog in a crowd, and it is essential when crossing busy streets. That's where heeling should end; it's boring for Duchess, and although all dogs should learn to heel, they should be given more freedom whenever the situation and space will safely allow.

Stop or Halt

This can be a lifesaving command. As soon as your pup has adapted to a collar, teach her to stop on command. Lessons are fundamental.

1. Walk to a door; when you open it, she will try to dash through.
2. Apply firm pressure to the training collar and give the command *"Stop."*
3. Repeat this training whenever you leave a car, reach a curb, and elsewhere until her obedience to the command is instantaneous. Rewards are given the same as before.

Obedience Rules

To acquire a personal copy of the AKC Obedience rules, write to the American Kennel Club at the address found in Useful Addresses and Literature on page 183 or visit the AKC website at *www.akc.org*. These rules will specify the height of jumps, the number of points awarded under various circumstances, and the way in which these points are accumulated toward the various titles.

Obedience trials use many rules to govern the conduct and appearance of competitors. For instance, dogs that have had plastic surgery to correct a congenital defect may participate in Obedience trials providing those dogs have also been neutered. Spaying, castration, mismarked dogs, or coat defects won't prevent dogs from participating in Obedience trials. However, lame or bandaged dogs may not compete, and dogs that have been dyed or artificially colored are ineligible.

Dogs that are not under the control of their handlers or handlers that abuse their dogs will be excused from competition. Handicapped handlers may compete in Obedience trials under modified rules. Their dogs are required to perform all the usual exercises, but the rules are bent to allow handicapped persons to exhibit their dogs.

When you and Duchess have mastered your early Obedience work and have graduated to Utility classes, there are some other home schooling techniques you might wish to try.

Utility classes involve exercises requiring Duchess to make scent determination. Scent training can take months to accomplish under the best circumstances. In order to succeed, you need to be resourceful and have the ability to find an approach that works for you and Duchess, then stick with it.

To establish your dog's confidence in the performance of any task, train Duchess in such a way that she can't be wrong. In the Utility class, she is required to locate a scented article from among several other identical, unscented articles. She must pick up and retrieve the article with your scent.

Your job in training is to be absolutely sure no other article in the exercise has your scent.

- Boil wooden dumbbells and air-dry them.
- Place them in a clean box that has been boiled to remove any existing scent, or in a new plastic bag.
- Handle them with boiled tongs or sterile latex gloves.
- Begin with only one clean article.
- Fix, fasten, or tie the unscented article securely to the ground, so she can't possibly pick it up and retrieve it.
- Wearing boiled or sterile latex gloves, fasten the clean dumbbell to the ground or to a large piece of plywood with heavy string, wire, or large staples. The string, wire, or staples should be devoid of all scent as well.
- Be sure the scented dumbbell is well saturated with your scent. Carry it around with you for a few days; rub your hands on it after playing with

Duchess. It should reek with your scent and that of your dog.

While holding Duchess nearby, place the scented article about a foot (30 cm) from where the clean article is fixed to the ground. Be sure the only article she can move is the scented one; then give her the command to fetch the scented dumbbell. If she touches a clean article, it must be replaced with another clean one before repeating the exercise.

Since she is able to pick up only the scented article, she will do so, return it to you, and receive her reward. Repeat the exercise using identical props. After she has repeatedly gone straight to the scented article a few times, move the scented article closer to the unscented one.

When she has mastered this step, increase the number of fixed clean articles. Add one clean article at a time, being sure it doesn't carry any scent and is fastened rigidly to the ground. When she consistently picks the scented dumbbell and returns it to you, add another. Gradually work up to about six unscented articles, but place only a single scented one among them.

The next step is to tie down the unscented dumbbells with a looser cord or wire, giving them more slack, but be sure she can't remove them from their mooring and bring them to you.

This rather simple, generic method for scent training will assure Duchess's success each time she is sent to fetch the scented article. It is impossible for her to be wrong, and she will soon make the association between the scented article and your praise.

9 *Agility Training*

Agility History and Appeal

Agility contests were first held in England in 1978 and came to the United States in the early 1980s. In 1986 the United States Dog Agility Association (USDAA) was founded, using the British format and course obstacles. Agility has spread to most of Europe, Australia, and New Zealand. An enjoyable contest to watch, this endeavor measures Duke's willingness to work with his handler and his versatility in a great number of situations.

Agility is as much a hobby as a competitive sport. Many German Shepherd owners who have no intention of entering their dogs in formal Agility trials find themselves caught up in the enjoyment of these good-natured contests. Agility appeals to bored dogs and their equally bored owners, bringing both to new heights of relaxation and dog appreciation. Training him in the rigors of Agility is a confidence builder for you and Duke. Many people have found Agility training to be a means of working out attention and focus problems with their dogs.

Although formal AKC-licensed Agility trials are open only to AKC-registered dogs, mixed breed dogs and their handlers frequently attain expertise. This sport, without AKC sanction, is being used more and more to establish a mutually acceptable training ground for both dog and handler. Dogs failing to perform well in Obedience work are often quite comfortable doing Agility. They seem to appreciate their freedom to express themselves under less stringent judging.

Agility is used as a diversion during tracking or search and rescue training as well. The purpose of Agility is to train Duke to accomplish certain feats, and since he is allowed to do this in his own way, he adds his own style and flair. As in Frisbee, many "hams" are found in the canine population as they respond to audience cheers and applause.

In 1990 the USDAA started awarding Agility titles earned in trials held under their sanction. Agility Dog (AD), Advanced Agility Dog (AAD), and Master Agility Dog (MAD) titles are earned and may be added to your dog's registered name. The USDAA awards titles to mixed breed dogs as well as registered purebred dogs.

Advantages of Agility Training

Agility training helps condition dogs for other tasks such as Obedience. As in other off-lead sports, the dog's response to the handler's commands and signals make this a sport of well-behaved, obedient competitors. It's a vigorous contest, second only to Frisbee in energy expended. To participate, Duke must be in top condition.

This is a sport similar in some respects to Obedience trials. In purebred dogs, it doesn't discriminate between pet-quality and show-quality dogs. If Duke is physically sound, trainable, and intelligent, he can probably excel in Agility. He won't be penalized for his long coat, undershot jaw, or short legs. Undersize Shepherds or those with light bones and long legs aren't seriously considered for placement in conformation shows, but are usually great prospects for Agility. The scourge of floppy ears may give him a teddy bear appearance and stop his show career before it gets off the ground, but "down

ears" won't constrain him in Agility work. Naturally, since dogs are worked off leash, Duke must have a biddable temperament and amicable personality. Some obedience training is necessary before he is worked in a common arena with other dogs. Qualities favoring winning in the sport of Agility are balance, concentration, and a definite desire to please. If those are among Duke's qualities, he may excel.

Trials

As an AKC-sanctioned event, Agility trials are divided into basic levels and more advanced competition. To enter, dogs must be at least one year old and registered with the AKC. Spayed bitches and neutered males are eligible but lame dogs or those wearing bandages are not allowed to enter. Off-colored dogs or dogs with unrecognized coat types or markings are considered equally with AKC Champions.

Titles and Awards

There are divisions and classes for handlers and dogs at every stage of training. The titles earned are Novice Agility (NA), Open Agility (OA), Agility Excellent (AX), and Master Agility Excellent (MX).

In order for Duke to earn the titles NA, OA, AX, and MX, he must acquire qualifying scores in three separate trials under two different judges. One title must be earned before the next level of competition is attempted. The MX title is earned after a dog has been awarded the AX title and has received qualifying scores in ten

separate trials. When earned, the title abbreviation is added at the end of a dog's registered name.

Obstacles

Agility trials use many props and obstacles sized according to the height of the dog. There are both broad and high jumps, an A-frame to climb over, an elevated dog walk to traverse, a teetering seesaw to walk or run across, a table to pause on, and an open tunnel to go through. There is a closed tunnel made of fabric that Duke must push his way through, a set of poles to weave through, and double bar jumps to leap over. There is also a suspended window he must jump through, a tire jump, and an identified area of the ground where he must pause.

In AKC trials, the obstacles are laid out on a course, and the handler runs along beside, behind, or in front of the performing dog. Handlers may not touch the dog at any time. The scoring is based on the course length and the time taken to complete it. A time penalty is charged for minor infractions. A refusal to try an obstacle counts five points against the participating dog. Refusals are not permitted for dogs competing in the AX class.

Importance of Concentration

Obedience trials have an aura of reservation, a silent, expectant quality. Hoopla and excitement are kept to a minimum and usually only follow the awarding of placements. Crowd noise is held to nominal applause and an occasional murmur. Herding trials are usually very quiet so dogs can easily keep their concentration. The same is true in freestyle dancing. Applause from the gallery is delayed until the performance is finished.

Agility trials, however, like Frisbee and Flyball contests, are spectator sports. They are held in enclosed arenas or open fields, and draw a large gallery. Probably the greatest problem encountered in Agility dogs is the fear or apprehension of performing in a strange place, off lead, with dozens of barking dogs and crowds of whistling, shouting people cheering their favorites.

Concentration or focus on you and on the task at hand is the premium quality of an Agility dog. If Duke has superior powers of concentration, an acute focus on you and the exercise, and is not easily distracted, he should do very well.

You must fine-tune Duke's concentration so he will look to you for signals, and concentrate on your commands. When he demonstrates the desirable focus, reward him amply. To maintain his concentration, don't overwork him, never let training exceed his attention span, and

make training enjoyable for both you and your dog.

The Keys to Successful Agility Training

Do not allow Duke to make the same mistake over and over. If he insists on hopping off the side of the dog walk or seesaw, put him on a short leash to control him. Hold his collar, if necessary, to impress him with the necessity of walking to the colored end before he jumps off. It may mean repeating the exercise several times, with rewards when he gets it right and not so much as a word when he makes mistakes. Don't scold him or physically reprimand him for any of his errors. Repeat the task, making sure he understands what you want from him, and reward him when he performs it correctly, whether he is on a leash or being held by his collar.

After you physically cause him to accomplish the exercise correctly a few times, and have duly rewarded him, discontinue training on the exercise and go to some other task, one he has already mastered. As in all training, Duke should always end his training session on a positive note, with an exercise he is sure of, even if it is walking on a leash once around the yard. It is important that he remembers that each training session ends with a special reward.

If Duke is exasperatingly slow to catch on, or if he doesn't seem to be getting the hang of things, look carefully at your methods. A normal German Shepherd should accept training readily and master tasks quickly. Before you get angry with Duke, ask the advice of a successful trainer. Join an Agility club; slow down and rethink your technique. Go to the library for a book on Agility training or buy one. In other words, look in a mirror; the problem may be yours, not Duke's.

Training for Trials

This is the time to enroll in a class if you haven't done so already. As mentioned earlier, you can construct the various obstacles, dog walks, pause tables, and A-frames yourself, and you can train all individual exercises without the benefit of an Agility club.

However, Duke must master all the obstacles one after another, according to your verbal commands or signals. He must perform before a noisy crowd of people and dogs and all sorts of strange sounds and odors. This will only come naturally to a dog with extraordinary concentration on his trainer for guidance. To obtain the needed experience, rely on an Agility club.

A Final Note on Agility

Agility is fun for participants and spectators alike, and if you have an active Agility club in your area, attend a trial. The participants universally enjoy themselves, yet the training both dogs and handlers undergo is extensive. If you have a biddable Shepherd, one that loves to please, Agility work may be for you. For more information, contact the AKC or the United States Dog Agility Association at the addresses and websites found on pages 183–184.

Home Schooling

Agility training should be carried out with a snug web buckle collar, and a short, light-weight leash. Some food rewards may be necessary, but, as in other training, their use should be kept to a minimum. Some trainers keep a small plastic bag in their hand containing the rewards to keep the dog's attention riveted to the signal hand.

Since many of the obstacles and equipment used in Agility are inexpensive to build, and many of them are collapsible, training can begin when the pup is quite young.

Contact obstacles include the dog walk, A-frame, crossover, and seesaw. They are so called because the ends of each obstacle are painted a contrasting color, and to score in a trial, the dog must touch or contact the painted end with at least one paw as he jumps on and off the obstacle.

Come. Puppies destined for Agility titles must learn the *come* command early, and it must be reliably performed without hesitation. In training, voice and hand signals should be given simultaneously, so Duke will not only focus on your hand signals, but will listen for your voice commands.

Hand signals. There are no standard commands for training; any one- or two-word direction to Duke is OK. He will identify the word with the desired action and with the hand signal. Hand signals should be given with the open hand, fingers held tightly together and extended rigidly.

Point your flat hand and fingers at the obstacle, and command Duke *"Take it," "Jump," "Over,"* or *"Through."*

Don't wave or make sweeping motions with your hand. Give the hand signal in the same way voice commands are given: directly, methodically, and without explanation or flourishes. Don't shout your verbal commands, but allow your excitement to accompany each hand signal and your voice.

Regulation Equipment

Write to the AKC for a copy of *Regulations for Agility Trials* or print a copy from the AKC website.

A-frame. A regulation A-frame can be built from two pieces of plywood, hinged in the center. Lay it nearly flat on the ground with the center elevated only a few inches by a brick lying sideways. Coax Duke back and forth across it. Initially, he will try to jump off the obstacle at will, but with positive enticement he will soon run across it on command. Reward him only when he crosses the obstacle from end to end, never when he jumps off the side.

Dog walk. Cut the plank to full regulation size, but leave it on the ground and encourage Duke to walk the entire length, getting on and off the plank only on the colored ends. When he has conquered this feat, raise the plank. Don't concern yourself with speed when teaching Duke how to approach and master each obstacle.

Seesaw. A seesaw can also be set up with a low center fulcrum in the beginning,

gradually raising it as Duke gets older and more confident. Verbal encouragement should be given as he makes his way along the obstacle, with excited praise being reserved for the times when he performs the task successfully.

Try to keep him focused on staying on the obstacle. Use your hand or, if necessary, his leash or a morsel of food.

Tunnels. Tunnels may be a problem until Duke has become accustomed to walking on plastic surfaces. Put a flat piece of plastic on the floor or lawn, one with the feel of an Agility tunnel. Encourage him to walk on it by offering a tidbit. Once he realizes this surface isn't to be avoided, the open tunnel or pipe tunnel should be a breeze.

If he is reluctant to enter a bent tunnel, set the open tunnel on a straight course and have a friend hold him at one end. Go to the opposite end and call to him. If necessary, crawl into the tunnel a short distance and coax him with a treat. A few such trials should relieve his fear. When mastered, the pipe tunnel can be bent in various directions.

Closed tunnels or collapsed tunnels present a problem for most young dogs, but they can be left until later, when Duke is more focused on his job. If you wish to train a pup to go through a closed tunnel, simply add a few feet of floppy cloth material to a short pipe tunnel. If possible, crawl through the tunnel ahead of him the first time or two. Once he realizes that all he has to do to open the tunnel is push his nose against the fabric, he will take this obstacle right in stride.

Jumps. Actual hurdles and jumps of all types should be reserved for when Duke is older. However, the *jump* command can be taught to very young puppies when they approach a two-by-four lying on edge on the ground.

Minimal height jumps can be set up for practice. It's best to erect sides to the barrier, so Duke must jump or stop. To encourage him to take a jump, give the command as you toss his favorite retrieving toy over the low jump, or through the tire jump. If this doesn't work, put him on a 6-foot (1.8-m) leash and walk beside him as you lead him to the jump. Give him the *jump* command, and encourage him up and over with gentle upward pressure on the leash as you jump the barrier.

10 *Herding*

The German Shepherd Dog is one of the oldest known herding breeds. Long before any of their other talents were discovered, they were used for tending cattle and sheep. They were excellently suited to this task, and their dedication to their flock, as has been mentioned previously, earned them the dignified title of Shepherd, instead of simply a "sheepdog."

Although one doesn't usually connect herding instincts with companion animals, herding abilities and guarding aptitudes are among the traits that make the German Shepherd so valuable as a family pet. Shepherds often can be depended on to keep the children of the family gathered together and under surveillance. Stories are common about Shepherds saving youngsters from many different types of household disasters, ranging from falling into a pool to wandering into the woods. When Duchess is with her children, woe to any molester or kidnapper who happens by!

Although in recent generations Shepherds have been bred more for show and for duties other than herding, they are placed in the AKC Herding group for good reasons. The Border Collie and Australian Shepherd are recognized by many to be the premier sheep and cattle herd-ing dogs, but they aren't the only ones that possess these talents.

Herding Instinct Certification

A herding instinct test is not a contest between several dogs, but is a pass or no pass test to demonstrate Duchess's innate ability and desire to herd livestock. It is a two-part test offered by Herding clubs to an individual dog, and if she passes, she may tack the title HIC onto her name. This test doesn't require any preliminary training or work and is open to any dog in the Herding group. Failing dogs may be retested another day.

Duchess will be given a "herd" of three cattle, sheep, goats, or ducks to work. She works with a collar or harness, and a leash, which is dragged. She can be handled by her owner or, in some cases, by the judge who is doing the testing.

She qualifies and earns the HIC when she shows a sustained interest in herding the stock furnished. She may circle, gather, or drive them for a period of time appropriate to evaluate the dog. In order to pass, she must show no viciousness and not make threatening gestures to the stock. A little barking and nipping is allowed, providing no actual "gripping" is done.

If Duchess shows uncontrollable aggressiveness, or if she displays no interest in the stock and doesn't try to work them, she fails the test.

A herding test gives the Shepherd owner a clue about the dog's interest and her inherent ability in handling stock before spending time and money preparing for Herding trials.

Herding Training

Herding training is geared to the dog's instinctive skills, which vary according to the breed and the individual dog within a breed. Training is done with appropriate livestock. There is basically no "home schooling" without livestock and sufficient pastureland to accommodate the stock. Instead of giving you hints about

starting Duchess on the way to Herding trials, we can only offer you some ideas about finding the means of training.

Many German Shepherd Herding clubs are active across the United States, and AKC Herding clubs and the American Herding Breed Association allow German Shepherds to run in their trials.

The courses are similar, the judging and scoring are subjective, and if Duchess is skilled in handling livestock, she should receive a fair evaluation. Dogs generally are graded on their outrun, lift, fetch, driving, and penning skills.

Dog-educated livestock are as important to training a stock dog as are other dogs to watch, observe, and help.

Maneuvers and Herding Terms

The outrun or cast is the maneuver in which the dog is sent to the herd. It means running in an arc, moving from the handler to the balance point on the far side of the stock.

The balance point is a position on the far side of the herd where the dog has the most influence on the herd and can best control the herd's movement.

The lift is the maneuver of the dog to gather and begin moving the stock toward the handler.

The fetch is the movement of the stock in the direction of the handler and pen.

Driving is the movement of stock away from the handler. In some contests, both

a right drive and a left drive are used. The livestock are usually driven through at least one gate during a drive.

Penning is the placement of the stock through another gate and into a pen.

Points

Herding trials are highly competitive and points are awarded according to the judge's placement. The number of points awarded to each dog depends on a number of factors, including the number of dogs competing in the class. Title awards also depend upon the particular breed club sponsoring the trial.

Herding Program and Titles

The AKC also sponsors a herding program for registered dogs in the AKC Herding group. This includes noncompetitive tests for dogs with some prior herding experi-

ence as well as competitive trials for dogs with training.

The title Herding Trial Dog (HTD) or Herding Trial Dog Excellent (HTDX) is awarded after earning qualifying scores given by two different judges in each of an intermediate and advanced class. The Herding Trial Champion (HTCh) title is awarded to a dog that earns sufficient points in class trials.

The American Herding Breed Association also awards HTD I, HTD II, HTD III, Junior Herding Dog (JHD), and Farm or Ranch Dog titles to dogs that earn qualifying scores in trials.

In AKC competition, three titles can be earned: Herding Started (HS), Herding Intermediate (HI), and Herding Excellent (HX). When Duchess has passed one level three times, at three trials, under three different judges, she may compete in trials of the next level. Five placements are awarded points in each of the levels. The ultimate title is the Herding Championship (H.Ch), which is awarded according to a formula considering placement in the classes and numbers of competing dogs.

11 Scenting

What Is Scenting?

Scent is defined in *Webster's New World Dictionary* as follows:

"To smell; perceive by the olfactory sense. To fill with an odor." (*vt*)

"To hunt by the sense of smell." (*vi*)

"A smell, odor, or the sense of smell. *An odor left by an animal by which it is tracked* in hunting. *A track followed in hunting.*" (*n*) (Emphasis added.)

As you can see, there is an overlapping of definitions. Scent, smell, and odor are words that are similarly defined. There seems to be no clear distinction among them, and under some circumstances, the three words are synonymous.

When speaking of dogs and tracking, we commonly use the word "scent" as a noun. It is an esoteric property of man and animals that is difficult for humans to perceive, but quite real to the dog.

Scenting is a verb used to describe a dog's ability to follow scents, *odor* is a noun used to describe a property more easily recognized by humans, while *smell* is a verb and is used synonymously with *sniff*, or it is a noun synonymous with *odor*.

Scenting Ability

Scenting ability might be defined as the competency of a dog to detect and follow another animal or to identify a particular substance by use of the dog's olfactory powers.

Since they are born with their eyes sealed shut, dogs learn to use their scenting ability to find their mother, her mammary glands, and even to locate a particular nipple. At a very early age, scent discrimination is already apparent and at work. Puppies first perceive humans through their olfactory system and can recognize strangers even before they are seen.

Olfactory sense, or the ability to smell and differentiate odors, is similar to the sense of taste, and is possessed in varying degrees by all mammals. Some animals are gifted with greater scenting ability than others, and domestic canines are among those species with the best-developed olfactory aptitudes. Wild cousins of the domestic dog probably have developed an even more discerning sense of smell than *Canis familiaris* since their lives often depend upon this ability.

Some breeds of dogs have more acute scenting proclivity than others. Perhaps this is because the sense is used more, or maybe olfactory capacity has been a major criterion for selective breeding. It is a well-known fact that some dogs within a breed have greater scenting talents than others of the same breed.

That the dog possesses a great olfactory ability hardly needs to be expounded upon. A greater percentage of the canine brain is concerned with the sense of smell than in the human brain. Dogs have 40 times more olfactory cells than humans. We've all heard stories of dogs' ability to detect minute amounts of gas escaping from buried pipelines. Newspapers carry reports of dogs locating humans who have been buried by tons of snow or the smoldering rubble of explosions. Escaped convicts are often found after being tracked for dozens of miles by a dog.

Scenting ability is present in all domestic canines, but it goes unused by many dogs. Those pooches aren't particularly interested in scent trails, and are content to merely fine-tune their scenting ability to detect special odors coming from the kitchen.

Even the laziest male dogs have been known to pick up the scent of a female in heat as far away as two miles, yet these same dogs have no apparent interest in following other scents. No doubt the reason for some dogs' lack of use of their scenting ability is their lack of need. They don't have to follow their "prey" since their food comes from a bag. Perhaps those dogs' lack of appreciation and development of their natural scenting ability is due to a lack of training.

What Is "Animal Scent"?

Most odorous substances are organic and heat increases their volatility by breaking the odors into small particles that become airborne.

There are two general types of scent, ground scent and airborne scent. Airborne scent is the body odor falling from, or swept from, an animal's body, which is carried by air currents. All animals produce some body odor, and each odor is characteristic of a particular animal. This odor might be likened to a very personal vapor enveloping the animal all its life. Airborne scent is concentrated near its source. It follows air currents and becomes more dilute the farther it travels.

Human body odor is a strong scent and is used for scent determination in Utility classes of Obedience trials. The scent of a human is made up of oils from sebaceous glands of the skin, natural skin debris, sweat, breath, and perhaps a *pheromone*. Pheromones are chemical substances secreted externally by some species and serving as a stimulus to others to elicit behavioral responses.

Human scents or body odors vary greatly among people and may reflect a person's race, diet, hygiene, toiletries used, and other components unique to each individual. The combination of these scents is the means by which your dog recognizes you, even in the dark. Long after Duke's vision diminishes due to the cataracts of old age, he can follow you by using his olfactory sense. Body odors are the major components of a track that remains behind when a person walks through an area.

Cold ground tends to hold scents in place, while warmer ground causes the scents to rise and diffuse more quickly. A snow-covered track is easier to follow than one laid on warm ground on a cool

morning, when the ambient temperature is considerably cooler than the ground temperature.

Scent concentration begins to dissipate and fade soon after the person has walked by. It diffuses in every direction due to the dynamic tendency of air to dilute and equalize the concentration of vapors. When a person passes by, his airborne scent is the first to leave, then his body odor, and finally, his track scent (defined on page 112).

Scent Cone

In nature, air is always on the move, but to understand airborne scent, you might think of a cone.

To demonstrate this scent cone, let's first imagine a hypothetical smoke bomb lying in a vacuum where there is a total absence of air movement. In such a case, the smoke never leaves its source, and the air immediately adjacent to the bomb becomes saturated with smoke. Smoke would become more and more concentrated at its source, but none would exist away from its source.

Imagine the same smoke bomb in a natural setting. The smoke source is now positioned on the ground in an open field. Imperceptible air currents carry the smoke away from the bomb in a three-dimensional pattern in the form of a cone. The smoke is quite concentrated at the source—the tip of the cone—and becomes increasingly dilute as it travels from the source. Higher wind speeds carry the smoke faster and the smoke cone becomes less dense as the distance is increased from the source, but the smoke from the bomb is continually produced, and the cone is always there.

Now imagine a human who assumes a stationary position in a similar spot. The human's body odor, which is continuously being produced, produces a similar cone. A dog's instinctive scenting ability involves more than the ability to detect the presence of an odor. Duke can also recognize the density or concentration of a scent and can instantly distinguish this scent from the hundreds of other scents in the area. Once the sought-after scent is perceived, he moves into its scent cone and follows the odor from low concentration toward high concentration; just how he does this is only conjecture. When he has followed the scent cone to its source, he has found the human or object being sought.

Airborne scent of a person is generally detected when the person is upwind of the dog. When an individual has passed through an area, his scent will be carried by breezes to ditches, water, trees, and other naturally occurring objects. It tends to cling to these objects for a time, then gradually is carried away by the wind.

If the human target is moving, the scent cone shifts with the person's movement. It will be distorted as the person changes directions, but the cone is still present. The dog's ability to work out the highest concentration of scent becomes quite difficult unless he uses other scenting abilities. This is why our immediate objective is to train Duke to keep his nose down, so he follows the *track scent*, and not the scattered airborne scent, which may be deceiving.

Track Scent

A moving animal leaves its track scent, which becomes more dense as the tracking dog nears the tracked animal. In the case of a human, this person's odor continuously sheds from the body, falls, and combines with the odor of shoes and clothing. Some of this scent is stamped into the soil, mixing with the odor of trampled ground cover. This cover is made up of broken grasses, twigs, and leaves, which lie in indentations in the surface of the soil. This mixture of smells becomes the person's track scent. Without realizing it, a complex track like no other has been left behind, following wherever the person goes.

Track scent is more apparent when the temperature is cool and rising, and when dew is evaporating during the early morning hours. A light rain following the laying of a track will freshen the scent and make it more easily tracked. Track scent may remain for hours, or even several days, when the weather is foggy, misty, and windless. Under those conditions, scent will slowly rise from the track and remain a few inches above ground. Hot weather, especially a hot, dry wind, will drive track scent away within a short time.

Scenting Is Natural

When walking with Duke in the country, you will introduce him to a variety of scents. Flowers, wild dill, wild onions, sage, and numerous other strong scents will interest him. The scent of broken grass or other crushed vegetation is perceived quite differently from the same plants that remain intact.

Squirrels, chipmunks, rabbits, humans, and various livestock leave tracks and track scents as they move through the pasture. Watch Duke's reaction when he finds a track, which you will identify as depressions in the ground made, for instance, by a cow passing by. He will immediately perceive the difference between the smells of growing plants and those of the same plants that are crushed by the cow.

Take him for walks in strange places. Watch to see if he picks up scents of animals and people from their tracks. You may see his "memory" of scents displayed; that is, he may follow the fresh scent of a rabbit, then interrupt this tracking to investigate the scent of a horse that passed by an hour ago, then return to the fresher rabbit scent, and continue tracking.

Allow him to track anything of interest to him and observe his head carriage, his ear set, and other distinctive body signals. These signs of his should be stored in your memory bank to be used later when you begin training.

Remove his leash when you get to the country. If you are not ready to trust him off lead, or if there is the possibility of danger to him off lead, buy a long retractile leash that will give him greater mobility. Although an off-lead walk in the country may not seem like a training exercise, it is indisputably one of the best ways to introduce your puppy to scenting and scent games. At the same time, it provides you, the handler, with body attitudes and signs you can use when his real training begins. You will see him prick his ears at certain scents, become excited at others, show a little fear at some, and display intense curiosity at a few.

Scent Games to Play

Your German Shepherd puppy is a bright, intelligent creature with tracking abilities you can hardly fathom. Duke's continual desire to play can be used to great advantage by substituting a learning game instead of a game of catch. Elementary training by means of simple games can begin in a very casual way when Duke is a weanling puppy.

113

Home Schooling

Your Dog's First Scent Game

It is natural for your Shepherd puppy to follow your personal scent. You are always with him; therefore, your scent is always around him, allowing him to find you quickly when you hide from him. Without realizing what he is doing, he picks up your scent, moves toward the highest concentration, and within seconds he knows which way you went and approximately where you are.

Finding the person with whom he has primarily bonded is a natural early type of tracking. Evidence of tracking ability usually shows up in very young Shepherds. If you have a large backyard, you may see Duke sniffing various tracks he encounters there. By these tracks, he learns every family member's scent, and differentiates yours from the others.

To test his scenting ability and discrimination, simply wait until he is preoccupied chewing a nylon bone or eating, then walk nonchalantly by him, and proceed to a good hiding spot. Have a family member or friend watch out a window, when you call Duke's name once.

At first, he may run around, using his eyes and ears to seek you, but when he is unable to find you by use of his hearing or vision, he will resort to his more acute olfactory sense. He will put his nose in the air, sniff, and soon, he will be standing before you, looking for his scratch and "*Atta boy, Duke!*"

As soon as he has shown the propensity to seek you out, you have already begun elementary tracking training. At this point scent training is nothing but a game, a continuation of hide-and-seek.

1. A friend holds Duke where he can't see you. You go to some secluded place in the yard out of sight and softly call his name once.
2. The friend lets him go, and he seeks and finds you. When this happens, make a grand show of affection and praise for his accomplishment.
3. Then the dog is held while you make a more circuitous route to a hiding place, and you don't call to him. The friend simply tells him "*Find Polly.*" If he shows a gift for seeking and finding, buy a tracking harness and a tracking line and continue.

Identity Games

Little games you play with Duke while he's a puppy are actually a beginning for search training. When you hide Duke's favorite nylon bone behind your back and ask him "Where's your bone?" you're teaching him the identity of the toy and training him to use his scenting ability to locate it. When he finds it, praise him effusively and let him know he did well. Each time you play this game of hide-and-seek with him, he learns something new about using his inherent olfactory capabilities.

You must intensify Duke's reasoning ability. When he brings you a ball, take it from him, but don't throw it. Ask him instead to "*Bring your bone.*" At first this command won't mean a thing, but when you have led him to his toy box and taken out the nylon bone, tossed it for him a few times, and told him each time to *"Fetch the bone,"* he will identify the word *bone* with the object.

Another time, when he brings his bone, take it and tell him *"Get the ball,"* and follow the same plan of object-name recognition training. Soon he will be able to identify each toy by its name.

Make a big issue of hiding his ball under a throw rug or behind a door. Then tell him *"Find the ball."* When he goes directly to it, praise him, tell him *"Good dog."* Hide it in several other obvious places around the house and repeat the exercise.

Then test his ability to differentiate one toy from another. Hide both his tennis ball and his nylon bone in an open closet or in another room. Tell him *"Find your bone."* If he makes the connection, and picks up the bone, lavish your affection on him. If he makes a mistake and picks up his ball, tell him in a conversational tone, *"Wrong, bone."* Then pick up the bone and hand it to him. Continue this game using only the bone. On another day, repeat the game using only the ball, then on a later date, try the differentiation exercise again.

Search Games

Progress from vision activities to scenting activities.

1. Have a friend hold Duke at the edge of the field, while you run into the field, calling to Duke as you run from him, then hide behind a tree or lie down in the tall grass.

2. Your friend tells the pup *"Find Polly,"* then releases Duke.

3. The handler follows Duke as well as possible, encouraging him to *"Find Polly."* In all probability Duke will race to you and lick your face.

4. It is important for you to run, not walk, to your hiding spot. Running away from the pup, like calling his name, will excite him and he will want to follow. Your object is to teach Duke to follow you to a place where he can't see you.

5. Repeat this game two or three times daily for a week, making your hiding places more difficult each day.

6. Switch roles with the handler. You might find Duke a bit reluctant to follow your friend into the field, but if he is into the game, it will only take a bit of encouragement for him to give it a go.

7. Hold Duke at the edge of the field, while your friend runs, calling to Duke. As soon as the friend drops out of sight, release Duke and tell him *"Find Ralph."* Then run alongside Duke, repeatedly telling him to find Ralph to let him know you are also playing this game. Duke should race to Ralph, and both Ralph and you should lavish praise on the dog.

Hide in more secluded spots and double back when running away from Duke. Change patterns—make the game more difficult each day. Keep each game short and simple but not boring. Don't play scenting games for more than a half hour per day, preferably less. Intersperse a previously mastered game, a walk in the park on leash, or a game of Frisbee.

12 *Tracking*

Tracking Equipment and Supplies

If you expect to begin tracking training, there is certain equipment you must purchase:

- A nonrestrictive, padded tracking harness for Duchess. A walking harness won't do; neither will a draft harness, as either may restrict the action of Duchess's shoulders and apply pressure to her neck when she is leaning into the tracking line. The chest piece of the harness should be padded and the harness should have adjustable fore-straps and hind-straps, so it can grow with Duchess. It should be lightweight and, above all, it should be adjusted to fit the dog. You should be able to comfortably place two fingers under all straps of the harness when it is properly fitted.
- A tracking line 40 feet (12 m) long, made of lightweight cotton webbing about 1/2 inch (1 cm) wide. Tie knots in this line at 10- and 20-feet (3- and 6-m) intervals.
- Several leather "articles" to drop. Possible articles include your old worn-out glove twisted into a roll and secured with a rubber band, or an old billfold you have carried, or your old discarded belt, doubled a few times and held with a rubber band.
- A few nonleather articles for future use: a handkerchief that has been carried in your pocket, a cotton glove you have worn, your old, worn canvas tennis shoe, one of your unlaundered socks tied in a knot, or a small paperback book you have read.
- Looking ahead, you should also purchase three 1/2-inch-diameter (1-cm) dowel rods, 3 to 4 feet (1-m) long, to use as flags. They are used to mark the starting point and the direction of the track. They should be topped with bright orange or red flags 12 to 15 inches (30–34 cm) square.
- During training, each turn is marked with longer dowels, which are not topped with flags. These markers are often painted dull black, with the upper 4 inches (10 cm) of the sticks painted white or orange. The white stakes might designate a right turn, the orange ones a left turn.
- It's always a good idea to take a suitable pan and a supply of bottled drinking water for you, your tracklayer, and your dog.
- Your tracklayer should be furnished with a clipboard and felt-tip marker to map the track when it becomes more complex and longer.

owner know you won't climb fences, and will take care of the fields as if they belonged to you. Find out if you will be allowed to train any time, or only when no livestock are in the field. Assure the landowner that Duchess won't chase livestock, and the presence of livestock won't interfere with Duchess's training. If the ideal spot found is located on public land, you must contact the agency controlling use of the land and get permission to enter and train your dog (see page 137).

Other needed items will become apparent when you get into Tracking contests and the competition continues in spite of bad weather conditions.

Country Training

This is a good place to mention location. Appropriate training areas are hard to find. For this training, it's best to have various open fields, trees, and ground cover to use. Usually this means you must go to the country for practice. If you find an ideal cow pasture, or other type of field, always contact the owner first. Introduce yourself and explain what you wish to do and how you will proceed. Give the owner your name, address, phone number, and the times you wish to use the property. Promise to close all gates, and let the

Scent Tracking an Article or Object

In tracking training, your object is not to teach Duchess to detect the "presence" of scent; this is an innate ability she already possesses. Your goal is to cause her to use her instinctive gifts to follow a given scent, moving from the lowest concentration of scent to the highest. In other words, you are going to teach her to discern a certain scent to the exclusion of more interesting smells she may encounter. Your plan is to teach her to use her scenting ability to find some object, and identify it by sending a signal to you; she must do this with minimal use of her vision or other senses.

A working bird dog is a perfect example of innate, discriminate scenting, and it also exemplifies the dog's concentration, which accompanies this ability. A bird dog in a field can undoubtedly smell dozens of interesting scents, including many other birds, but the scent she seeks is that of a game bird.

Home Schooling

The first stage of training takes place in your backyard. Put Duchess' tracking harness on her and have a friend hold her. She should not, however, be held by the tracking line. The tracking line is to use only when on a track, and is an easily abused tool. Instead, the "handler" should hold Duchess by putting an arm around the dog's chest.

You are going to be the target of Duchess's tracking. Leave Duchess's sight, go around the house in one direction, then double back and hide in the opposite direction. The handler releases Duchess and tells her "*Find*." She will first depend on her vision to look for you where she saw you last, then will wise up and use her nose to find you. The handler follows her, holding the line attached to her tracking harness. When she has successfully found you, both you and the handler should lavish praise and affection on her. Repeat this exercise two or three times daily for several days.

In the next stage of her home-school tracking education, you can lay tracks for her to follow in an accessible field, preferably one with trees, tall grass, and other diversions.

1. Set two flagged stakes, about 20 feet (6.1 m) apart. While the handler is holding Duchess, scratch her, make a fuss over her, and show your affection.
2. The handler then takes Duchess to a place where she can't see you. You walk to the starting stake, trample down the grass in an area about 3 feet (1 m) square to the right of this stake, and walk, dragging your feet, to the second stake, which you pass on the right.
3. Walk, taking short steps in a straight line, to a point perhaps 20 paces distant.
4. Hide behind a tree or lie down in the tall grass. The handler then takes Duchess to the starting flag and has her lie down with her nose in the trampled grass area.
5. Call Duchess's name one time. The handler tells Duchess "*Find Polly*." She then follows behind Duchess, keeping just a little tension on the tracking line.
6. Duchess probably will look about, then race in the direction of your voice. When she can't see you, she will begin tracking you to your hiding place. If she falters or deviates from your scent track, don't hesitate to call to her again. At the same time, the handler will gently return her to the straight track you have made, and in a normal voice again tell Duchess "*Find*." If you are well hidden, you may need to call her name several times. To avoid confusion and to keep Duchess's attention on you, the handler should not use Duchess's name when she is guiding her back to the track. This type of game-playing sets the stage for more intense training.

Never force Duchess to track. Neither this very elementary tracking nor the next stage of training described in the following text should be mandated to her. If she is a little off one day and seems reluctant to play your game, pull up the stakes and quit. She may be suffering from a simple malady affecting her olfactory system, and she may not feel like tracking. Wait a few days before beginning again.

A Bird Dog's Body Language

The body language displayed by a Brittany working in front of her handler indicates whether she is on a cold trail or a hot scent. When she picks up a faint quail scent on the wind (the outermost reaches of the scent cone), she stops quartering, her head drops lower, her ears perk, and with her nose close to the ground, she moves in the direction of the strongest source of one specific scent. The instant she detects the presence of a recent quail track, she hesitates briefly, then lifts her feet one at a time, moving slowly forward until she is certain. She then freezes with her nose pointing at the invisible covey of quail. A slight movement of her flagging tail tells her handler she is serious; the birds are just there.

The bird dog uses her body language to tell her handler:

1. She is searching or casting about for a scent.
2. She has picked up the scent of a game bird and sorted it out from all other scents.
3. She has tracked her quarry to a specific spot.
4. She is identifying the quarry and is holding it.

Likewise, a tracking dog instinctively sends signals to her handler with her ear set, head position, shoulder movement, and tail. The expressions of a tracking dog's appendages tell the handler whether she is tracking a scent or casting (searching) for a given scent. They may also indicate how concentrated the scent

is and how sure the dog is of the track. When the end of the track is located, and the article being tracked is in view, she responds by sitting, barking, lying down, picking up the article, or retrieving it.

A Dog's Tracking Mechanism

As stated previously, no one fully understands the mechanism a dog uses when tracking. We don't really need to know the answer to this technical question to help a dog learn to use her inherited tracking ability in a certain manner. The objective in tracking is to encourage the dog to concentrate on a given scent and follow it until an object or article is found. Moreover, in tracking, the scent she is to follow is the ground scent, not the wind-borne scent.

Humans' Olfactory System

Tracking may seem impossible to teach when we consider our own weakness. The human olfactory system seems to be flawed, since we can't begin to follow a human scent. This is because of our relatively small number of olfactory cells and our propensity to become "immune" to or tolerant of certain smells. Humans become accustomed to odors in a fairly short time. Have you ever smelled a more enticing odor than that produced by a batch of big, gooey chocolate chip cookies baking in the oven? Bakery workers are robbed of this heavenly experience; after the first day, they can't even smell them.

Example: Cattle pastures surrounding our veterinary hospital emitted their own particular smell. The odors from these pastures didn't offend me; in fact, I was oblivious to them until I returned from a vacation, then for a few hours, I smelled the cattle and their manure. By noon, my olfactory sense had adjusted to these odors. I had effectively tuned them out and they were no longer perceived. They might become apparent again after an early morning dew or when the sky cleared after a light rain has fallen.

Dogs' Lack of Immunity to Scents

Dogs apparently do not become accustomed to any scents; at least the propensity is not generally manifested. A well-trained tracking dog will trail a given scent for extended periods of time without becoming "immune" to it. It remains sharp in her memory, and if the trail is interrupted time and again, she will still be able to pick it up and follow it.

Serious Tracking

Tracking is a standardized sport, one that owners and dogs alike can enjoy. Dogs can be started tracking at about four to six months old; those trained in this sport show great enthusiasm and eagerness to participate. Tracking, like Obedience, is a sport that can be pursued on a formal basis.

Once the fundamentals of tracking have been mastered, you must continue training Duchess during every type of weather and in every kind of terrain.

Tracking Dog Contests

Complete rules for AKC Tracking contests are available in booklet form from the American Kennel Club or from the AKC website (see page 183 for the address). They are condensed here for ease in reading.

- A stranger to Duchess lays the track out following a line that has been plotted by a judge.
- Certain articles belonging to you and depicted at the beginning of this chapter are randomly dropped on the track by the "tracklayer," so they can't be seen for more than 20 feet (6 m), nor can they be covered with anything to hide them.
- Duchess is kept on a line and the handler follows her at a distance of no less than 20 feet (6 m) except in heavy cover.
- Verbal commands may be given by handlers to encourage her, but the handler can't indicate the location or direction of the track.
- There is no time limit on the track. However, if she stops working the trail, she is marked failed.

Levels and Awards

Tracking Test/TD is for dogs more than six months old that have not yet earned a Tracking Dog (TD), Tracking Dog Excellent (TDX), or Variable Surface Tracking (VST) title. The TD title is earned when a dog is certified by two judges as having passed a Tracking Test/TD.

The TD requirements include the following criteria. The track followed must be at least 440 to 500 yards (402–457 m) long, with each leg of the track at least 50 yards (46 m) long. The track must be 30 minutes to two hours old. A total of three to five turns are used, including both left and right turns. Specific rules govern where turns may be made, the degree of the turns, and any fences and boundaries that may be included in tracks. Parallel tracks can't be used, and the proximity of other tracks is also governed by TD rules, as are the obstacles that are allowable in TD tests.

A Tracking Test/TDX is available to dogs that have already earned a TD title.

The TDX title is awarded to dogs that have been certified by two judges to have passed a TDX test.

In TDX competition, the length of track is increased to between 800 and 1,000 yards (732–914 m), but the length of each leg remains at 50 yards (46 m). The track age is increased to three to five hours old, and five to seven turns at various angles are used. Crosstracks, obstacles, and specific articles are included in this test to increase its complexity.

VST verifies the dog's ability to recognize and follow human scent while adapting to changing scenting conditions. Each track has a minimum of three different surfaces, including vegetation and two areas devoid of vegetation such as concrete, asphalt, gravel, sand, hardpan, or mulch. No obstacles are used in this test, but tracks may be laid out through distractions such as buildings, breezeways, shelters, and open garages.

There are four articles used in the VST test, each of which is made of a material different from the others, and all of which may be easily picked up by the dog. They are leather, plastic, metal, and fabric.

Certificates of TD, TDX, and VST are awarded by the AKC to the dog when certain qualifications are met. It's a competitive sport, but not in the same sense as Obedience trials or conformation showing, since no points or placements are awarded.

As in other canine contests and events, there is camaraderie among Tracking dog handlers, win or lose, and Tracking contests are pleasurable events to attend as a spectator as well.

If you wish to compete in this sport, your first step is to contact a Tracking club, and get professional help through their trainers and handlers. They will furnish the expertise and equipment needed, and will offer valuable advice every step of the way. If there are no Tracking clubs nearby and you decide to try to train your dog in this discipline without professional trainers, the results can still be very rewarding.

The Pace of Tracking Training

It's important to understand that you can't hurry tracking, nor can it be forced. A dog forced or compelled to comply may keep her nose to the ground only to avoid a handler's abuse. She may fake scenting the track. At the very least, forcing a dog to work will diminish her desire to work without direction, which is the object of tracking.

No two dogs are alike and each will progress at her own pace. Duchess may be a great tracker and may progress quite rapidly, or she may be just average, but no more than an hour a day should be devoted to this training. Don't push her! Some dogs are so caught up in tracking they can handle training every day; for others, the training should come less often, perhaps two or three times a week. Your dog will let you know if you are giving her more than she wants. Her enthusiasm and excitement will wane, and she will become reluctant to work.

Positive Reinforcement

If you are given to verbal scolding or physical corrections when your dog doesn't perform well, you might rethink this habit, or rethink your tracking plans. For instance, Duchess's inability or lack of desire to follow a track may be a sign of nasal irritation or a medication that has affected her olfactory organs. If you get upset when she seems reluctant to follow a track while training, you take the chance of ruining a good dog.

As with other training, positive reinforcement of correct actions will win the day. Praise in your tone given for satisfactory completion of an exercise will be remembered, and Duchess's actions will be repeated. Once a proper response is received, the exercise should be repeated and through practice and repetition it will become second nature to the dog.

Duchess must learn that when the tracking harness goes on, and the command "*Find*" is given, there is actually something out there to find. She must learn to follow the tracklayer's track scent, which always leads to the object. Motivation is the key to starting a dog to track. Get your dog stimulated and eager by your voice modulation, your actions, the tracklayer's voice, and his handling of the article to be found. The first time Duchess finds the article, show her your elation. Talk to her; jazz her up for the exercise, then don't allow her to become bored by repeating the same exercise more than a couple of times each training day.

If you have not taught your dog anything more than good manners, she can be taught to follow a track. Obedience training is not a prerequisite to tracking; in fact, you may find training easier if your dog hasn't mastered formal obedience work. Great patience is required to teach your dog to track, although once the fundamentals are mastered, it may seem as if your dog is the teacher and you are the student.

To recap: Tracking is a sport or exercise to be enjoyed by owner and dog in an

informal way, just for fun. The aim of the trainer is to slightly modify the natural scenting behavior of the dog. The training should be gradual and systematic, and should be taken seriously, but should never include physical or oral reprimands. Obedience commands aren't used in tracking training, except perhaps the *down* command before starting the course or when the article is identified.

Dog Mistakes

Confusion About Your Role

When Duchess is still a puppy, her most common mistake might be associated with confusion when you begin to act as handler and you first ask her to follow someone else's scent. If that happens, simply switch roles; let your friend be handler and *you* lay the track. Don't rush her. She will catch on in her own time.

Owner Versus Article

Another early problem might be encountered if she doesn't understand the connection between tracking to find her owner, and tracking to find a glove. If she is less than anxious to follow a stranger's track to the glove the first time, simply take her over the track to the glove, point to it, and when she picks it up, lavish praise on her and play with her and the glove for a few minutes. If it doesn't work, switch roles and lay the track yourself.

Sensitivity to the Tracking Line

Duchess might be sensitive to the tracking line and may not track well against a taut line. Most handlers prefer a taut tracking line, but it isn't absolutely necessary for successful tracking. Some dogs won't work on a taut line, but will track all day on a slack line. Don't force Duchess to lean into the line if she objects to doing so. She will probably learn to pull into the line when she gains confidence in her performance.

Stopping

Stopping on the track is another undesirable habit, but if the stops are brief, and if she continues to follow the right track after she has stopped, there's no need to be concerned. It's natural for Duchess to stop and sniff a crosstrack made by a squirrel or a cow. If Duchess feels the need to defecate or urinate while tracking, no correction is necessary; the habit can usually be resolved by taking her for a little walk in a familiar "toilet" area prior to the tracking exercise. However, excessive urination or urinary marking shouldn't be tolerated. A soft, verbal "*No*," followed by the gentle command "*Find*" is usually sufficient to remind her that she is here to track, not to mark.

Losing the Track

If Duchess loses the track and doubles back to you, point to it, direct her along the track, repeat the command "*Find*," and try to excite her about finding the article. If you have used the find command frequently when playing with her and tossing the article, she is not apt to forget what it means.

Trailing

Trailing is another tracking error in which the dog follows body odors or airborne scent, instead of track scent. You can identify a trailing dog by a higher than normal head carriage. She may hold her head down when following a scent with the wind, but carries her head higher when tracking into the wind. This is not your goal, but you should not lose confidence if the beginning dog is guilty of this practice. Continued training, longer tracks, and greater motivation of the dog to find the article will usually resolve this error.

When an experienced tracking dog is performing well, she keeps her nose to the ground for several paces, then raises her head, exhales, and resumes. After she has found the direction of the track she will raise her head slightly and check the track scent every few paces. This body attitude comes only with practice.

Fringe Following

This is an error in which the dog moves into and out of the track, crisscrossing it in a snakelike manner. It is usually caused by scenting airborne odors instead of the track scent. The fringe-following dog will usually "quarter" and sniff the breeze with her head up, rarely putting her nose to the ground. A fringe follower often overruns turns in the track. She will usually come to a turn, begin to circle to the right, then, with luck, may find the track scent and continue to follow it.

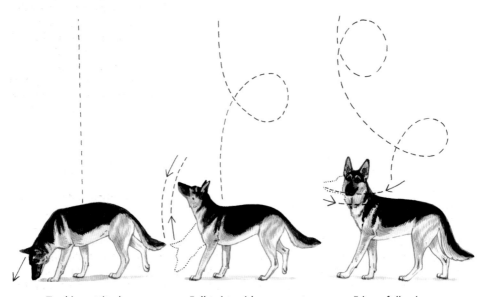

Tracking attitude · Following airborne scents · Fringe following

Refusal to Track

Some dogs remember their early obedience training too well. Duchess may take a *heel* position and refuse to leave it. She may ignore the *find* command, since it hasn't been taught to her. To help alleviate this problem, take her to the country where she can be exercised and allowed to investigate track scents off lead. Exercise her in the woods where she hasn't been before and take along her retrieving bumper, tossing it for her in an informal way.

The next time you go to the country, take a small leather article, and get your Shepherd accustomed to retrieving it. Let the obedience training fade into the back of her brain, and concentrate on the article she likes best. Each time you toss it for her, tell her *"Find,"* then lavish affection on her when she reaches it and picks it up. Follow this with the elementary tracking exercises previously described wherein a friend holds her and you hide from her.

Track Turns

When Duchess has grasped the idea of tracking and is advancing well, turns, or corners, in the pattern of the track should be instituted. This usually occurs some time during the third week of training. At first, square corners should be used; later, as your confidence in her ability increases, other turns can be included in the track.

1. The tracklayer begins as if laying a straight track. At the point where a turn is to be made, the tracklayer stops, and a *turn stake* is planted on the opposite side of the track from the direction in

which the track is to continue. In other words, when turning to the left, the stake is planted at arm's length to the right of the track, and if turning right, the stake is planted at arm's length to the left of the track.

2. After planting the turn stake, the tracklayer should turn 90 degrees and continue walking while dragging or shuffling his feet to make the track at the turn more obvious. The turning stakes may also be color-coded on the top. For instance, a yellow-topped stake might mean a right turn, and an orange-topped stake a left turn, or vice versa. The stake will tell the handler which direction the tracklayer has taken, and on which side the tracklayer passed the stake.

3. The tracklayer continues walking until the designated distance has been covered. He then drops the article directly on the track, steps on it, takes another step past the article, and plants the article flag in the ground. This will not only mark the direction in which the track goes, but also the location of the article.

4. The tracklayer then takes another 15 to 25 paces past the article and exits from the field in a circuitous manner.

Handling Articles

Many times, other members of the family, friends, or onlookers are present during training. Don't allow them to touch the article to be used. The person(s) whose scent is on the article should always be of primary interest, since this is the basis for every exercise of this sort. The scent of the dog's owner-handler is always on the article. The only other scent on the article should be that of the tracklayer, the target person who is involved with laying the track for the dog. Duchess will easily differentiate her handler's scent, and if her handler is behind her, she will understand that it is the other scent to be found. If it is possible for any other scent to be on the article, don't use that item in a tracking exercise.

When training a new dog, the tracklayer should carry the article in direct contact with his skin. Sometimes, to increase the concentration of the scent, the article is carried under the tracklayer's upper arm to assure that the article will be well identified with him. The tracklayer should always carry the article in the same manner.

Stepping on the Article

This is another important part of tracklaying. Placing a foot on the article increases the scent on it and pushes it into the ground cover so it is more difficult for Duchess to locate visually. It is also easier to locate by scent, since stepping on it crushes vegetation under it. In training, the article should not be covered up.

Later, stakes (except for the starting flag and direction flag) are no longer used, and natural markers serve this purpose. These natural markers might be a clump of flowers, a stand of dead grass, a stump, a branch, or other objects. These are lined up, noted on the map, and used to hold the track in a straight line from point to point.

Handler's Duties

Most Shepherds can be taught to track, but in order to do so, the handler must

have patience and acquire and practice certain skills. In the beginning, the handler must motivate Duchess by playing with her with the article she is to find. Early in training, the tracking harness is worn by the dog, and the article is seen by Duchess in the hands of the tracklayer until it is dropped.

As soon as Duchess has begun to get the hang of this program, the handler should alter her actions. She takes Duchess to the field with a collar and leash. She then removes Duchess's collar and the tracking harness is buckled on when she is taken to the starting stake. There she causes her to lie down with her nose smack in the middle of the trampled grass. Soon, Duchess will make a connection between the harness, the tracklayer's scent at the starting flag, and the article she is expected to find.

If Duchess doesn't immediately identify the track scent when she has reached the starting stake, the handler allows her to lie there for a short time, then the handler touches the track and gives Duchess the *find* command.

As Duchess picks up the scent at the starting stake, the tracking line should be played out in a certain way.

1. The carefully coiled line is gripped in the handler's left hand, and is held behind her body.
2. The line is gradually played out and is slid through the handler's right hand, which is held in front of the handler's body and high above her head. She should be careful to keep slight tension on the line, and care should be taken so it never touches the ground between the handler and dog.

3. When her left hand feels the first knot at 10 feet (3 m), the handler begins to move with the dog.

4. When the second knot is felt at 20 feet (6 m), passing through the left hand, the handler grips the second knot with her right hand and wraps the line around her right wrist.

5. The handler must keep up with her dog and keep the line taut and free from tangling. The line is held above her head to be sure it doesn't become tangled if Duchess stops and circles. If Duchess stops, the handler should also stop immediately so as to maintain the integrity of the track. If Duchess comes back toward the handler, the line should be taken in with the handler's left hand and dropped to the ground in front of her. The handler then restarts the dog on the track by touching the track in front of her, and giving the *find* command. As Duchess proceeds on the track, the line should be played out with the left hand, until the line becomes taut once again.

6. When Duchess has advanced to working tracks through brush, tall weeds, and trees, the handler should gradually take in the line to the 10-foot (3-m) knot, still holding the line above her head and keeping the line taut. The handler should never jerk the line, but keep steady pressure on it so that Duchess is leaning into her harness.

7. When Duchess has completed the track and identified the article, the handler should praise and reward her. The handler should then remove Duchess's harness and lead her from the field with her collar and leash, which have been carried in the handler's pocket. This way, Duchess identifies her tracking duties with the tracking harness, and knows the exercise is finished when the article is found and the harness is removed.

More Tracking Terms

Track age is another variable tracking dogs must contend with. In early training, all scenting is done on very fresh or recent tracks. Later on, the track age is varied, with some being 15 minutes, others an hour or two old.

Track faithful, or Track sure is the term applied to a dog that tracks with such intensity nothing seems to interfere with her concentration.

Track happy is the term describing a bouncy, fun-loving dog with little commitment to tracking, a dog with a short attention span and minimal concentration.

A linetracker is a dog with the desired tracking behavior. In her early training, this dog will watch for the article dropped by the tracklayer, mark this spot, run to the marked place, and use her nose to find the object. This is the dog that quickly learns to locate and follow the track scent to the article.

Steptracking dogs are those that move slowly along a track, moving their heads and shoulders as they proceed from one footprint to the next. This action is especially valuable when the track crosses pavement or hardpan and there is no crushed grass or weeds in the track.

Home Schooling

The following discussion is not meant to take the place of formal training under the tutelage of a professional dog trainer with expertise and experience in AKC Tracking contests. Instead, these ideas may help you start your dog in the sport, give you some of the terminology used in Tracking, and prevent the errors that are made most often.

The Track

When we refer to the sport of Tracking, we must surely have a track. The track is the path a tracklayer has taken, and it ends with an article that is dropped by the track-layer. When the track is laid out, and the article has been dropped, the object of the exercise is to convince our Shepherd to follow the track and identify the article. In the beginning, the proper laying of a track is an important part of the sport of Tracking.

The Tracklayer

The tracklayer is the person who lays out the track, which means that a second person is required in this teaching exercise. The tracklayer may be a family member with husband and wife or teenage child assisting, or another dog owner who is interested in the sport. In formal contests, the tracklayer is a stranger to the dog, but that formality is not necessary at this beginning stage of training.

Before you start, before you ever go to the tracking field you have chosen, discuss thoroughly with your tracklayer just what his job is. If one of you has previous experience with tracking, so much the better, but if not, be sure you have gone over the following details thoroughly. Sometimes it is best to rehearse tracklaying a few days before the dog is introduced to the field.

Rehearsal

Early in the training process, when a short, straight track is being used, mapping isn't necessary. But when the track is longer, contains turns, hills, obstacles, and other complications, a map must be made. The tracklayer draws this map, which may include where and how far each natural object is that pertains to the track. The map is important to show the handler exactly where the track lies, and to enable the handler to keep Duchess on track.

Laying a Track

An early spring or fall morning is the best time to begin tracking training. Summer is OK if you live in a temperate climate, but training shouldn't be started if the weather is hot and dry.

The area should be free of distractions such as curious livestock or moving machinery. A field of grass standing 3 to 6 inches (7.6–15 cm) tall is ideal. Choose an area that has a number of visually discernible natural objects rising above the ground cover. These natural objects might be stumps, branches, patches of flowers, clumps of tall weeds, posts, trees, or any other object easily visualized, which will help the tracklayer line out the track and keep it straight. The tracklayer plants a starting stake, selects a natural object in the distance, and walks *in a straight line* toward the object.

The first track should be about 5 yards (4.5 m) long, but this short track should be extended to a distance of 150 yards (137 m) or more by the end of the first week of training. As the distance becomes greater, the tracklayer should line up two objects, one about halfway to the second. By keeping these objects visually in line, the track should remain straight.

In the rehearsal, the tracklayer determines the wind direction and selects the visual objects before anything else is done. Following a line between these objects must lead the tracklayer into the wind. He then plants the 3-foot- (1-m)-tall starting flag in the ground and tramples down the grass over an area about 1 yard (1 m) square to the immediate right of the starting flag. Starting from this trampled area he walks in a straight line toward the chosen natural object in the field. He takes short steps and drags his feet. When the tracklayer has gone about 5 yards (4.5 m), he continues for another couple of feet and plants the *article flag*, which is another stake just like the starting stake.

He then makes an "about face" and calls to Duchess (Duchess isn't at the rehearsal, but this should be practiced anyway). After gaining Duchess's attention, the tracklayer tosses the article up and catches it a few times, then makes a big production of throwing the article to the ground in front of him. The tracklayer then steps on the article and returns to

NOTE: *This discussion is meant for home schooling only, and contains information applicable to slower dogs. You will find that professional trainers rarely use double- or triple-laid tracks today. Double- and triple-laid tracks were popular before the advent of TDX training, because, in the TDX degree, the dog must decide in which direction the track leads. If you intend to compete in formal TDX competition, please omit all references to double- and triple-laid tracks. Most German Shepherds will follow single tracks from the very beginning. If you find this to be true for Duchess, you should omit all multiple-laid tracks.*

the starting flag, retracing his original track (double-laying the track).

It is important to be sure of the following.

1. The article flag is slightly beyond the article and planted directly in the track.
2. The tracklayer walks in a straight line to and from the article stake.
3. The tracklayer takes precisely the same track back to the starting stake.
4. As these training tracks are laid, the tracklayer should remember to shuffle his feet to crush the ground cover and leave the maximum track-scent trail. When this has been accomplished, you have the basis for all tracklaying except tracks with turns. They will be discussed later.

The First Day

A day or two after the rehearsal, take Duchess to the field. Put the tracking harness on her and adjust it to fit. Snap the line onto it, and play with Duchess with the glove or other article you have selected to be used in the exercise. Attempt to motivate her to watch and identify the article. Toss it for her to retrieve, and let her mouth it a minute before you take it from her.

When you toss the article, tell her "*Find*," then, holding the tracking line with a minimum of pressure, follow her and praise her when she picks it up, not when she brings it to you. Remember that you are trying to teach Duchess to track, not to retrieve. If she is already retrieving everything you throw, it won't interfere with her tracking, but remember the difference between tracking and retrieving.

After you have played with Duchess and the glove for a few minutes, have the tracklayer toss the glove a few times for Duchess while you hold the tracking line. When the glove is thrown, tell Duchess "*Find*," and follow her to the glove. Always keep a slight tension on the tracking line between you and the dog so she can feel you following, and you can feel her body movement. Praise Duchess when she picks up the glove, take it from her, and repeat this process. It is important to get Duchess well motivated to find the glove each time it is tossed. It is equally important to follow her, keeping the tracking line free from tangling, and to reward her with your praise for finding the article.

The tracklayer then tests the direction of the wind and chooses the spot he has selected as the starting point. Remembering the rehearsal, he plants the starting flag and tramples down 1 square yard (1 m) of grass to the right of the flag. Duchess is held at this spot while the tracklayer takes the article from you and proceeds five paces in a straight line, dragging his feet, and moving upwind. All the time the tracklayer is walking away from the starting flag, he should be tossing the glove into the air and playing with it, keeping Duchess's attention focused on the article. After taking the five paces, the tracklayer goes two more paces, plants the article flag, turns 180 degrees, and retraces the two paces. The tracklayer then calls or whistles, and when the dog has fixed her attention on the tracklayer, the tracklayer should toss the article up and catch it a few more times. When Duchess's focus is riveted to the article, it is thrown to the ground on the track. The tracklayer then steps on the article and walks quickly on his track to the starting flag. It is important for the tracklayer to walk past you, the handler, without touching either of you, and without saying anything to you or Duchess. He should step to the left of the starting flag, and continue a few paces.

Tell Duchess "*Find*" and release her. Hold the tracking line about 5 feet (1.5 m) from the dog. The slight tension you keep on the line is not meant to hold Duchess back, just to let her know you are there with her. If she wants to run, let her, and do your best to keep up.

At first, Duchess will use her eyes to mark the spot where the article fell, and

will use her scenting ability only for 1 or 2 feet (30–60 cm) at the end of the track to locate the article in the grass. As the track is gradually lengthened, she will rely more on her nose and less on her eyes to find the object. Eventually, when Duchess can't watch the track being laid out, she will be inclined to use her nose to follow the track.

After Duchess has successfully found the article, praise her, pet her, and tell her what a good dog she is, then repeat the exercise once at the same distance. The next step is to lengthen the track to 10 yards (9 m), following the same technique as before. This distance should also be repeated once. The third and final exercise of the day is the same as the first two, with the tracking distance increased to 20 yards (18 m), and repeated once.

Never forget to give Duchess lots of praise and ear scratching for her correct performance. Your approval is her reward for doing a good job. She should always be aware of your presence, close behind, when she finds the article. Take it from her if she picks it up. She should feel you on the other end of the tracking line and hear your gentle voice encouraging her as she advances to the article. Always assure her she is doing exactly what you want her to do.

It is critical for you to know precisely where the track is so that if Duchess deviates from the track, you can slow down and, with the tracking line, gently guide her back to the track. *Don't ever jerk the line or scold her*. If she is tired of the game after two tracks, don't lose your cool. Simply lead her to the article, point to it, and ask her to pick it up. Praise her for picking it up, then play with her or let her carry it as you walk home. She's still a good dog; don't forget to tell her so.

The tracking line should never touch the ground between the dog and the handler; there should always be a slight tension on it. As Duchess progresses, the line should be taut from the dog's harness to your hand, and Duchess should become accustomed to tracking against a certain amount of line pressure. On a taut line, the handler can better detect what the dog is doing, whether she is changing direction, slowing down, or speeding up.

If Duchess continues to try, and wants to please you, but hasn't caught on and doesn't perform in the way described, don't be upset. Repeat the exercise at shorter distances and, together with the tracklayer, try to excite and motivate Duchess to move quickly on the track to the article. Extensive playing with Duchess before the tracking exercise is begun can help. Toss the article and let her pick it up and mouth it before the exercise begins. Motivate her to find it when you toss it, reward her with ample praise, and always use an article with which Duchess is familiar. It is important for Duchess to end the training session with success and the usual reward.

Subsequent Days

In the following days the same exercise is repeated, but at longer and longer distances. The first track on the second day should be a repeat of the last track of the first day. The final track at the end of the second day should be double the distance of the first day's final track. The first track of the third day should be a repeat of the last track of the second day. The final track of the third day should be double the distance of the final track of the second day, and so on.

At this stage of training, the track is still laid in a straight line, upwind from the starting point, which is to help Duchess follow the tracklayer's scent instead of his visual appearance.

Longer Tracks

As the track becomes longer and Duchess isn't able to see the tracklayer drop the article, the tracklayer must remember to shuffle his feet along, dragging his heels to make the track very obvious. On long tracks, the tracklayer should drop the article on the track, step on it, proceed another few steps to plant the article flag, return on the track to the article, step on it again, and continue walking to the starting flag.

Ideally, Duchess should be following an upwind track of 400 yards (366 m) by the end of the first week. In the case of a 5-yard (4.6-m) track, it's easy for the tracklayer to follow a straight line; the handler knows exactly where the line is, and can bring Duchess back to the track if she should go astray. When the track is extended, it is necessary for the tracklayer to mark it better for the handler. This entails two slight changes in tracklaying:

1. The tracklayer takes two stakes with him as the track is laid out. He still lines up two natural objects to help maintain a straight track, but, in addition, as he passes the halfway point of the track,

the tracklayer stops and plants another stake in the ground about 1 foot (30 cm) or so to the left of the track. He then proceeds to the end of the track, takes two paces beyond, and places the article stake in the same manner as before.

2. He then turns 180 degrees and retraces his two steps to the end of the track. With much ado, he tosses the article in the air a few times and throws it to the ground, then, using the stakes as a guide, the tracklayer steps on the article and retraces his steps exactly to the starting stake. Immediately after the track-layer passes the handler, Duchess is sent to find with you, the handler, following.

During the first week of training, the primary intent is to instill in Duchess's mind the presence of an object, which is always out there when the *find* command is given. She will also realize that you, as the handler, always accompany her. You must follow the track precisely. This is important when Duchess needs to be restarted or if she leaves the track more than a few feet. When this happens, you must then begin to increase the tension on the line and eventually stop, bringing the dog back on the track.

Single Track

When Duchess has successfully found the article for several days following a double track, which is the one formed by the track-layer retracing his tracks to the starting flag, the track is reduced to a single track.

This is accomplished by the tracklayer who, after planting the article stake, drop-ping the article, and stepping on it as pre-viously described, continues for about ten paces beyond the article stake, then circles wide to reach the starting stake.

This reduces track-scent concentration and increases the difficulty of the exercise considerably, but it should be no challenge for Duchess. From the time your dog has begun to follow single tracks, the track should be alternated between single- and double-laid tracks. Triple-laid tracks can be used if Duchess doesn't do well on single tracks. As stated previously, double and triple tracks are rarely used by contem-porary trainers who are training dogs for competition.

Downwind and Crosswind Tracks

Once Duchess has successfully tracked for a week or so, the tracklayer should lay out the track by walking with the wind (in the same direction as the air currents are flow-ing). These downwind tracks are more dif-ficult because Duchess can no longer depend on scenting the tracklayer's air-borne scent, and must rely more on track scent (see page 112).

From this point on, the downwind and upwind tracks should be alternated on dif-ferent days, and by the end of three weeks of training, Duchess should follow either type of track with little difficulty. Now, a crosswind track should be laid.

A crosswind track is even more difficult for the dog because she must concentrate solely on the track scent, and not on air-borne scents, which move laterally across the track, with the wind.

13 *Searching*

The idea of teaching Duke to search for a lost child or an adult who has wandered away from home has great merit. Perhaps he may even save a child's life or safely return a disabled senior to a nursing home.

Like many other specialized duties we have assigned to dogs, more particularly to the German Shepherd Dog, search training is usually carried out under the tutelage of professional trainers. Those women and men who have successfully trained dogs and their handlers for specialty work should be consulted before you begin this training, unless you are simply looking for another practical discipline to occupy your spare hours and keep you and your Shepherd busy.

Permission First

Once again, remember that training areas are becoming more and more difficult to find. It's best to have various open fields, trees, and ground cover to use for this training. The well-groomed lawn of a city park doesn't fit the need and we must go to the country for practice. As stated before, when you find an ideal cow pasture, or other type of field, *contact the landowner personally, before you enter.*

Introduce yourself and explain what you are up to and how you will proceed. Give this person your card or at least your name, address, and phone number. If you honor property ownership, you will probably be welcome. The same holds true of public lands; all are under management of a city, county, state, or federal agency, from which permission must be obtained before the land is used.

Search and Find

This term is generally used to describe the activity of a dog that has been trained to search a given area to find some article a person has dropped. He will then follow the track scent until he discovers the person who dropped the article. It is a continuation of both tracking and searching tasks. This is an activity that seems to come naturally to some dogs, but is totally confusing to others.

Search and find combines the previously discussed tracking and searching exercises. In this exercise, however, no starting flags are used and there is no scent track laid for the dog to follow. The dog must first search for and find a scented article, then track its human owner to his hiding place.

In tracking and in his previous experience with searching, the dropped article was the object of Duke's endeavor. Finding the article gained him the reward he was looking for, your approval and praise.

In *search and find*, the article being searched for is only the beginning. He must then follow the track of the scent found on the article until he discovers the person who matches the scent.

Home Schooling

If Duke displays an interest in tracking, you might try training him to search on your own. Be very careful that you do not challenge his attention span. Be patient. Do not train for more than 15 minutes to half an hour per day. In search training, boredom and distractions are often a problem. If Duke displays apathy or a lack of focus during search training, call it a day and take him for a long walk.

Food rewards are important to Duke and are positive reinforcements that work well in most training. However, food rewards are rarely used in search training because he might be distracted by the odor of a bag of cooked liver treats in your pocket. Do not begin with food treats and then stop using them later in the training program. A better idea is to start your search training by using verbal rewards and stay with that plan. A few verbal *"Atta boy"* rewards and a quick pat on the head or a bit of chin rubbing will suffice. The appreciative tone of your voice and gentle touching are signs of your love and are all the reward Duke wants. If you play with him regularly, take him for walks in the country, let him investigate his environment, and challenge his brain with games and problems to solve, an occasional treat is all Duke will desire.

Some trainers advise practicing all training activities when Duke has an empty stomach. That is a great idea most of the time. Any dog will focus on the task at hand and work harder when he knows that feeding time is imminent. However,

if Duke has progressed to the point where he is being used as a trained search dog, he will likely try his best when looking for a lost child and succeed as frequently when he has just eaten as he will when he is hungry. During initial training, you should schedule his session before a meal if convenient. However, if you are planning ahead for a real-world searching activity, do not change either his feeding schedule or his training schedule.

Minimum Use of Obedience Commands

It is important to use a minimum of obedience commands and equipment when engaged in this type of training. If you take him to the field with a training collar, he will be ready to heel all the time and won't be anxious to search or find. If he is told to *stay* when a friend is holding him as you are leaving to hide, he will be undecided about running after you. He will wonder how long he should stay. If you shout for him to come when you have hidden, an adult Shepherd may become frustrated, and even bite the person who is preventing him from immediately going to your side. He is not apt to forget his obedience training, but to avoid confusion, you should devise an entirely new vocabulary for this and other similar endeavors.

1. Take him to the field with a web collar and a long leash, and forget the *heel* command.
2. Remove his collar and leash and have your friend hold the dog firmly in his arms when you are hiding from him.

3. Shout his name or whistle for him when you are hidden. When this signal is heard, he should be released immediately.

   Search and wait are commands to be taught in this training. Wait is used by the handler when Duke gets too far ahead of you and you aren't able to easily follow him, such as when he is working in heavy underbrush. In this regard, remember he is searching for a "victim" and if he's on a hot scent, he should rarely be restrained. If he returns to you frequently and you want him to keep his mind on the victim, use the search command.

   Down is about the only obedience command used, and will be discussed later.

Training to Search

The tone or modulation of your voice is quickly recognized by your dog. Try to use the same tone for the search, find, wait, or down command. A different voice modulation should be used to tell him "Steady" when he approaches the victim or "No" when he needs correction for dwelling on some animal track while working. Yet another tone of voice should be used to praise and reward him with a "Good dog."

Don't shout. Duke has far better hearing than you do, and shouting is usually perceived by your dog as disapproval. Let excitement come through your voice when Duke is nearing his quest in a search exercise. Give him lots of "Atta boy" rewards, and throw in a few "Good boy" and "Way to go, Duke" praises when he is trying hard.

Search training is not a continuation of tracking training, in that Duke won't have a track scent to follow. Search may be taught before, after, or instead of tracking. In this endeavor, your dog will rarely wear his tracking harness and line. Search is usually taught after tracking, because in tracking he learned to routinely follow scents to an object. In searching, Duke will also look for a familiar or foreign scent he knows is hiding from him.

For his safety Duke is worked without a collar because he will eventually be searching in heavy underbrush, which may snag on a collar and impede his progress. Since he will be on his own when he picks up the scent of the article for which he is searching, no restrictions are placed on him.

1. In the beginning, select an article small enough to throw, and one with which he is familiar. A small canvas dummy used for retrieving will work well. Some trainers choose to use a tennis ball instead. A tennis ball is of the correct size and is easily handled, but it has a disadvantage of being a common object to most backyards. Because these balls are so widespread, Duke may not differentiate between the ball being used and another he may find lying around. He may also connect the ball with playing catch.

2. Toss the dummy where it can be seen, and give him the search command. Already accustomed to retrieving, Duke will chase the dummy and probably pick it up and return it to you. It is important to give him a vocal reward when he reaches and identifies the dummy. As usual, reward him with lots of praise and petting.

3. Take the dummy from him, throw it again, this time into a less visible place, and tell him "*Search.*" Repeat this toss and search game no more than half a dozen times a day for a few days. When Duke quickly searches the area into which you have tossed the dummy, he instinctively realizes he isn't just searching with his eyes to locate it. When it is thrown a fair distance, it will scoot along the ground and disappear under leaves or in cover. He knows he must follow its scent and track the dummy. He sees it drop in a certain area,

searches for its scent, and its scent leads him to the dummy.

4. Progress from tossing the dummy to hiding it. This is easily done when he knows what object he is seeking, and the general area in which it is hidden. Have a friend hold Duke out of sight. Hide the dummy in the same general location where he has searched and found it previously, then call to him. Your friend releases him, and when the dog comes to you, tell him "*Search.*" If he fails to go to the area in which the dummy is hidden, pretend you are

throwing the dummy. If he still fails to catch on, lead him to the hiding place and point toward it, telling him "*Search*." When he finally finds it, praise must be lavished on him.

5. Next, the same exercise is repeated, but the dummy is hidden in other unlikely spots in the yard. Other articles, such as those used in tracking training, may be substituted for the dummy. Soon, he will identify your scent on the article when it is shown to him and will search for it. Once he has found the articles in every hiding place in the yard, he can be taken to various fields you have located previously. There you should first let him see you toss the dummy into the weeds and tell him "*Search*." When he understands what you want from him, toss various other articles for him to locate by searching.

Throw these articles in every direction so as to cause him to work upwind, downwind, and crosswind. Once he has mastered searching for and finding the articles thrown randomly around the fields, move to other areas and continue this practice.

Hiding Articles

Duke will soon become proficient in finding various articles that have been thrown in every direction in strange fields into various types of cover. At this point, begin "hiding" the articles.

1. Take the article into the field by bicycle or have a friend hold Duke behind your car so he can't see you as you walk in circles into the field, then throw the article as far as you can into cover. For this purpose, the retriever dummy is once again an excellent search article because it is saturated with your scent. It usually has a short rope tied to one end, which is used as a handle to throw it a great distance.

2. Return to your dog, and tell him "*Search*." He may immediately head into the field, but he may be confused because he didn't see you throw the dummy. You can often start him off by pretending to throw something, or you can point, or even walk with him in the direction the dummy landed. Once he picks up the scent of the dummy, he should home in on it and find it without difficulty.

3. The dummy may be "planted" or hidden in a field by a stranger or a helper who takes it out of sight and drops it. Under some rare circumstances, a vehicle may be driven into the field and the article dropped from the vehicle in some out-of-the-way place. Generally that is not an option, however, since few of us own land to be used this way, and it is a rare farmer or rancher who will give permission to drive a car over a horse pasture to accommodate dog training!

Home Schooling

Searching for You

Begin this exercise in the same way as all others. Make all conditions as simple as possible. Use an upwind direction, a recent track age, and short distances in the beginning. Progress to downwind, older tracks, and longer, more complicated distances as Duke becomes more proficient.

Just as in searching, when Duke is engaged in *search and find*, he will be working without his tracking harness or collar for safety reasons. The absence of his harness may disturb him initially because it was directly related to his training in tracking, but if he has been searching, it should present no problem.

At this point, you should realize you have an option of making this program rather easy, and by all means you should do so. It's been previously mentioned that the most familiar scent in Duke's memory bank is yours. He is always following you around by your scent; why not use it here?

1. Have a friend hold Duke at the edge of the field where he can't see you or what you are doing. To hold him, the handler should use his arm, or the end of Duke's tracking line placed loosely around his neck.

2. You are to be the "victim" in this exercise. Take a personal article—a belt you have worn, an old billfold, a canvas sneaker, or one of your leather gloves—with you as you go into the field.

3. Enter the field from the opposite side or a distance from where you are going to drop the article. Locate the prearranged natural object where you are to plant the article, such as a clump of tall grass, a rock, branch, or a small patch of flowers in the field. When you reach it, drop the article, then shuffle your feet as you make a right-angle turn and walk to a good hiding place.

4. Have your friend take Duke to an area near your entry into the field, release him, and tell him *"Search."* Typically, Duke will remember his earlier search training, and will immediately seek something with your scent on it. He may quarter closely, like a bird dog seeking a familiar scent, or he may race wildly into the field and begin to criss-cross it with his head raised to pick up airborne scents.

5. The handler should follow Duke closely and encourage him as he nears the place where your article was dropped. When the article is found, the handler should tell Duke *"Good boy,"* then command him *"Down,"* and pick up or take the article from him, praising him for a minute before buckling on his tracking harness and line. After allowing him to sniff the article he has just found, send him to find, exactly as would be done at the starting flag in a tracking contest. Hopefully Duke will remember his harness and the fun he's had tracking and will start off as usual with his interest drawn to your track scent.

6. Since he will be tracking a single-laid track, he may have a little trouble following it. If he seems to be experienc-

ing difficulty, the handler should encourage him to move in the correct direction. When he understands he is seeking something else, he has been told to find it, and it is your scent leading away from the article, he should move forward vigorously.

7. Duke is now in his harness and tracking the most familiar scent he will ever know. This leg of the exercise should therefore go quickly. When he discovers your hiding place, he will be elated. This is the first time he has searched for and tracked you. Your approval for his success should match his enthusiasm in finding you!

Repeat this *search and find* exercise daily for a week, then introduce a new twist to the endeavor.

Introducing a Stranger into the Exercise

For this exercise, someone Duke has never met assumes the role of "victim." He travels to the chosen field separately from you and your dog, and enters the field from a distant spot. The victim takes with him an article saturated with his scent, such as a sock or other article of clothing he has recently worn, which hasn't been laundered. This is dropped in the field in the prearranged search area, then he walks further into the field, 50 yards (46 m) or more, to a hidden area and sits or lies down well out of sight.

1. Take Duke to the search area and tell him "*Search.*" He may be a little con-

fused since you are standing there beside him, and each time in the past, you were the object of his *search and find* exercise. Encourage him by repeating "*Search*" a couple of times, and "*Come on, Duke, search for it.*"

2. Once he begins to work the field and quarter in front of you, he should have no problem locating the sock, heavily scented with the stranger's odors. Upon discovery of the article, tell him "*Down,*" pick up the sock, and lay it in front of his nose on the victim's track.

3. Buckle Duke's harness on him, snap the tracking line in place, let him sniff the sock, and tell him "*Find.*"

4. Follow Duke with a taut line, as you have done in tracking exercises. Encourage him as he homes in on the track scent, and when he tracks the stranger to his hiding place, gently tell him "*Good boy*" and "*Down.*"

A German Shepherd that isn't accustomed to encountering strangers under these circumstances may occasionally assume a defensive or offensive attitude. When Duke first becomes aware that the object being sought is a living person, he may bark excitedly, growl, snarl, or become frightened. Don't scold him, or encourage him to make a fuss. Assure him with your voice, gently tell him "*Down,*" and then stroke and praise him for a few seconds. Begin talking to the stranger in a comfortable, quiet voice. After verbally greeting the stranger, move slowly toward him in a friendly way, with the two of you touching, shaking hands, and laughing in a familiar manner.

Tell your victim ahead of time that when he is found, he should speak to Duke in a kind voice, but should not use Duke's name nor should he try to touch Duke until they have been introduced. As soon as Duke has regained his composure, speak to him, and introduce him to the stranger.

This exercise is repeated the next training day with a different victim being used in a different field. As training progresses, the tracklayer-victim may cross his own track and try to confuse Duke with its pattern, but Duke will see through these tactics and lead you to him.

These training exercises should be carried out in a variety of weather conditions with different track ages until Duke has learned *search and tracking* is no different than any other task.

Searching Without a Dropped Article

This training is more difficult because the scent being sought will be moving from trees, bushes, and grasses on which it was captured. It will be apparent on shrubs that the victim has passed. The scent will be found "hanging" in ditches or depressions, but it won't necessarily be impressed on the ground in the search area. It will be borne on the breeze and suspended in the still air of the woods.

This type of scenting is much like the activity of a bird dog that knows the smell of game birds, and will quarter and seek until they are encountered. Once a definite scent source is identified, the dog

will move toward the strongest source until a track scent or the victim is found (review the discussion of a scent cone on page 111).

The key to this exercise is Duke's recognition of a particular scent given to him, and his memory of the scent. When a dog can accomplish this feat, he is already half trained. The culmination of searching is reached when Duke discovers the victim or the person who is wearing the scented clothing.

In the early training, you are to play the role of victim once again.

1. You hide after entering the field from another direction. At first, you should enter the field from upwind and hide a short distance from the search area. Later, you should enter against a crosswind or downwind from the search area, and the distance of your hiding spot from the search area may be increased.

2. Once hidden, you should remain quiet unless it is obvious that Duke is having a difficult time, then a familiar whistle or a quick shout is sufficient.

3. The training is essentially the same as in the *search and find*, except in this case, Polly acts as handler and takes Duke to the prearranged search area. An article of your clothing, such as a worn, unlaundered sock, is given to Duke to smell when the search area is reached. Polly (the handler) then removes Duke's collar and tells him *"Search for Ralph* (the victim)." Hopefully, he will work the area until his trained nose picks up your airborne

scent. Every dog has his own method of searching for such a scent. Quartering like a pointer is quite acceptable, as is crisscrossing the area.

It is important to remember this is a training exercise. You should always begin with a small search area, with a fairly easily discovered hiding place relatively close to the search area. You want air currents moving from the victim toward the dog. In the beginning, it is best to use a pasture or field not inhabited by livestock. The fewer recent crosstracks and distractions Duke has to deal with, the better. And above all, don't forget to reward Duke heartily when he finds you.

The exercise is repeated once on the first day, and twice on the next training day, still keeping all factors simple and easy. When the search for you is successfully made on every try, increase the difficulty. Enter the field and hide in a difficult spot, one farther from the search area. Use crosswinds and opposing winds to make the search more difficult. The age of the scent should be gradually increased as well.

Searching for a Friend

This role switch is used after a few days of search training. Change roles with your assistant. You are now the handler, and Ralph is the victim.

1. Ralph enters the field from upwind and hides close to the search area.
2. Take Duke to the search area and let him sniff Ralph's unlaundered sock.

3. Tell Duke to search. He may be confused by the fact that you are the usual victim, and you are standing right beside him.
4. Show him the victim's clothing, encourage him to sniff, while repeating "*Search for Ralph.*"

If Ralph is familiar to Duke, his scent will be nearly as familiar as yours and the dog should have no trouble catching on. When Duke is no longer uncomfortable with a different victim, it is time to begin the final stage of searching.

Searching for a Stranger

In this exercise you must once again employ the services of persons who are strangers to Duke. The same method is used as in the previous discussion.

1. Begin with a well-saturated scent item such as a T-shirt or sock that hasn't been washed since it was worn.
2. Have the stranger enter the field from upwind and hide in an easily discovered spot not far from the search area.
3. You are the handler. Take Duke to the search area; show him the article, let him sniff it thoroughly, and tell him to search. At first, he will have you and Ralph on his mind, but once he realizes Ralph's scent is not present, and another scent is quite obvious, he should begin to quarter or crisscross until the new scent is discovered.
4. When he is obviously following a scent toward the victim's hiding place, reassure him with "*Good boy, Duke,*" and

lots of other positive assurances that he is doing just what you want.

5. When he nears the stranger, but before he confronts this person, tell him "*Steady, Duke*," in a normal tone of voice.

6. When he comes on a stranger who is obviously hiding, he will probably look to you for direction. That's when you tell him "*Down, Duke*" and go quickly to his side. Praise him and make a fuss over him for a few seconds, then place his collar on him, so he will realize the exercise is finished.

7. Greet the stranger and let Duke see you touching and shaking hands with the person. At this point, introduce Duke to the stranger and together leave the field.

From here, the exercises become more difficult in new areas. Lapsed time, winds, ground cover, and climatic conditions confound the problems. Once Duke has gotten the hang of searching an area for a scent, one to which he has been introduced in some manner, he is on his way to becoming a fine search dog.

14 Conformation Shows

What Is a Show Dog?

Some people say the conformation show ring ruins working breeds. Show rules and regulations standardize the appearance, temperament, and movement of members of a breed. They govern what colors are allowed, how the dog should be groomed, and what hair can be clipped. They dictate the maximum and minimum size for a breed, whether it should be fine- or coarse-boned, and how much muscle mass it should have. The dog's gait and build are specified. Conformation shows set the appearance standards and temperament qualities allowed in a breed. They are an accumulation and consensus of the fanciers of the particular breed who make up the breed clubs, and who create the standards.

A dog show brings uniformity to a breed. How can this be wrong? Usually, it isn't. In the German Shepherd Dog, a sincere effort has been made to combine natural beauty with innate intelligence, trainability, strength, movement, personality, and sound working ability, and to judge every dog entering the ring on all these fundamentals.

Unfortunately, judges rarely see beyond the general appearance of the dog, its coat, bone structure, angulation, temperament, and gait. They can easily see if the dog is the correct size and proportion, if it is strong enough to be an effective herder or guide dog. They can judge the expression, and those dogs displaying a kindly attitude and willingness to listen to their handlers are placed higher. They can pick a dog with an easy, elastic, yet strong trot with significant length to the gait to cover miles with little effort.

On the other hand, show judges can hardly be expected to take the dogs to the field and test their scenting abilities, their willingness, their devotion, their reasoning powers, or their agility. There is no test in a show ring to judge a dog's ability to move a flock of sheep. In short, show judges do quite well, but there is always room for error when choosing the Shepherd they think is the best representative of the breed from any given group of dogs.

All registered Shepherds can be entered in an AKC conformation show, providing they have reached the minimum age of six months, are physically normal, and have been trained sufficiently to behave in the ring.

Breed Standard

The Official Breed Standard for the German Shepherd Dog is published in the *AKC Complete Dog Book* and is also available from the German Shepherd Dog Club of America. Their addresses and websites are found under Useful Addresses and Literature, starting on page 182. Included here are a few excerpts from the standard.

The dog should be strong, agile, well muscled, alert and lively, deep-bodied, and substantial. Balance is also important. It must present a picture of fitness and nimbleness without any look of clumsiness. Its masculinity or femininity must be obvious.

A German Shepherd male stands 24 to 26 inches (61–66 cm), and a female 22 to 24 inches (56–61 cm), and both are slightly longer than tall. The Shepherd's head is not coarse, but chiseled and strong. The ears are moderately pointed, open toward the front, and carried erect. The muzzle is long and strong, and the nose rubber is always black. A scissors bite is preferred; a level bite or overshot jaw is undesirable, and an undershot jaw is a disqualifying feature.

The topline should be straight, with the withers higher and sloping into the back, which is neither sagging nor roached. The Shepherd's ribs are well-sprung, and not flat or barrel shaped.

Its abdomen is not paunchy, and only moderately tucked up. The croup is long and gradually sloping.

The saber tale is bushy and long enough to reach the hock, but should never be curled over the back. The dog's angulation, both front and back, is an important feature of judging, as is the musculature of its forequarters and hindquarters. The feet are short, compact, and well arched.

The dog's nails are black and should be trimmed neatly back. Its double coat is medium length and dense but should lie close to the body. A soft, silky, long, or wooly outer coat is a fault. Pale, washed out colors, blues, or liver colors are faults and white dogs are disqualified.

The German Shepherd is a trotting dog that moves with an outreaching, elastic rhythm, covering a maximum amount of ground with a minimum of effort. It characteristically has a powerful, coordinated stride that is well balanced, whether in a trot or walk.

Show dogs must be manageable and trustworthy, and trained in the exercises common to conformation shows, since control is a vital part of participation in shows. The Shepherd breed standard includes rather specific temperament characteristics. The desirable Shepherd is fearless but not hostile. It must exude confidence but not make immediate friendships. It must be approachable and willing to meet overtures. It should be eager and alert, and never timid or nervous. Shyness is penalized as a very serious fault and a dog displaying this trait must be excused from the ring.

Disqualifications include: cropped or floppy ears, a nose rubber that isn't

totally black, an undershot jaw, a docked tail, white color, and signs of physical aggressiveness toward the judge.

Handlers

A dog show is the only place where you can compete with professional handlers for the same trophies with absolutely no training or experience. You can enter the ring alongside men and women with years of experience, and sometimes, if you watch closely, show energetic enthusiasm, and have an outstanding dog with the qualities being sought, you can win in spite of overwhelming odds.

However, an owner or handler generally shouldn't try to exhibit a dog without the benefit of some classes and instruction. Shepherd clubs and all-breed clubs usually hold handler classes at least once a year. If a child has aspirations of handling the family dog in an AKC show, start the youngster's junior handling education early. While no preference is given to children-handlers, a well-dressed child who does a good job handling a fine Shepherd will quickly get the attention of the judge and the gallery.

Owners who are prospective handlers should first attend dog shows to see what is expected of them. When the judge tells the handler "Up and back," the reaction should be instantaneous. Sometimes, judges call their top dogs out of competition very quietly, and the handler must listen carefully. Nothing is more embarrassing than to have Duchess be the dog

chosen and not realize it until the judge shouts "German Shepherd Dog," to the gallery's amusement.

You, as a handler, must never upstage your dog. You must be able to hold Duchess's focus, give her cues, and coax her most bubbly personality from her without appearing to be on display yourself. The judge should always be looking at your dog, never at you. Nagging a dog is a serious handler fault, and *all* training should take place *outside* the show ring.

A handler's personal appearance is important; it should be conservative without flash or flair. No one present is interested in your clothes, and they shouldn't catch anyone's eye. Don't distract from your dog. Brightly colored vests or jackets, billowy dresses, high-heeled shoes, or gaudy jewelry call attention to you, and when worn in the show ring constitute grave mistakes.

The Gait

To gait Duchess, you must find her best-looking trot and, through practice, lead her precisely at this speed. It should be an easy gait, and should be launched and stopped quickly, with few, if any, verbal cues. If this sounds like she is in automatic drive, the gallery should think so. Your job is to train yourself to be consistent in all things in the ring. Duchess might be the finest German Shepherd Dog present, but unless she is shown to the judge in the very best light, she won't win.

You are in serious competition. You're going head to head with all types of handlers. Some are nearly unscrupulous in their methods; they may seem quite laid-back, but will beat you at their own game. Good handlers learn how to exhibit their dogs so as to show what the judges want to see, without letting those same judges see what shouldn't be seen. By manipulating gaits and stances, their dogs catch the judge's eye, and may appear more perfect than they are. Their nonchalant, automatic movements are practiced day in and day out, and are varied slightly to meet the personality of each judge. It isn't enough to have the best dog; you must learn to be a finely tuned handler to take home the purple. Only in rare instances is the dog's perfection sufficient to hide the handler's errors.

Entries

The AKC is particular about show entries. Everything must be in order on the dog's registration, and the application and payment must be correctly filed and mailed by a deadline date.

Judging

AKC judges mentally compare each dog in the class with the "perfect" German Shepherd Dog described in the breed standard. Allowances are made for age, maturity, and differences between the sexes. The judge must be conversant with virtually every point in the breed standard and make placements accordingly.

Conformation dogs are not judged on the basis of the breed standard alone. Judges have the responsibility to consider the dog's attitude and conditioning.

Training and willingness are important parts of showing, and dogs that are obviously enjoying themselves have a better chance at winning than those just going through the motions.

Types of Shows

To learn more about the specifics of AKC dog shows, write to the AKC for *Rules Applying to Dog Shows* or contact them by visiting their website, found on page 183.

Point Shows

These shows are governed by AKC rules, under the direction of a licensed superintendent. Entered dogs compete for points accumulated toward the coveted AKC Champion title.

Sanctioned Matches

These are informal contests at which AKC-registered purebred dogs compete, but no points are awarded to winners. They are often held by all-breed clubs to generate interest and give novice dogs and their equally novice handlers a chance to compete under show conditions. Training is an important part of these matches, and if you haven't tested your Shepherd's training, try it out here, not in a point show.

Fun Matches

Simulating shows or sanctioned matches are the fun matches held by clubs. Often called puppy matches, these competitions are usually the first exposure a dog gets to dog show discipline. This is the first place to see if the training you and Duchess have accomplished is sufficient to move ahead. Judging is informal and instructional, and clubs sometimes award ribbons for winners. No championship points are awarded.

Junior Handling

This is the place to start children on the road to show dog handling. Their dogs may be novices or champions. Handlers are competing against other handlers without regard to the dogs they handle. Obviously, the better trained the dog, the better the handler can look. A sure winner is a neat, well-dressed, self-confident youngster with a well-trained, exuberant Shepherd. Judging is meant to be instructional to the child, and in order to do well, the child should have practiced moving and working with the dog prior to show time.

Home Schooling

If you are planning a show career for your dog, before you begin, join a local German Shepherd Dog club and consult with Shepherd owners in your club. Have Duchess "faulted" or judged informally by someone who has been involved with the breed for a while and who has shown dogs. If the pup isn't sufficiently mature, or has an obvious conformational or behavioral problem, the experienced person should be able to point it out to you. This preliminary judging is not mandated, but it may save you a lot of heartache and expense.

If it appears that Duchess has the qualities to win, enroll her in showmanship and show training classes. Enter Duchess in fun matches for experience—yours and hers. If all goes well in the classes and matches, you are ready for the big time.

If you decide to enter your Shepherd in a dog show, you may elect to exhibit her yourself or hire a professional handler. A show dog and her handler must be trained. Duchess must obey you instantly, and she must look to you for direction. She should be trained to trot in front of you, but shouldn't appear to be pulling her handler

along. Duchess must be trained to stand and pose or *stack* for examination by the judge. She shouldn't be easily distracted, and must stand very still when the judge runs his hands over her. Duchess can't resent being handled by a stranger; the judge will also open Duchess's lips to expose her bite. The dog must accept these invasions of privacy with good nature, and a little tail wagging doesn't hurt her chances a bit.

Does this sound familiar? The training required for conformation showing isn't much different than elementary obedience training, good citizen, and good manners training. If you wish to handle Duchess yourself, and hopefully you will, review those sections of this book for instructions.

15 Guide and Assistance Dogs

Specialty and *handicap* dog training certainly isn't limited to the German Shepherd Dog, but Shepherds' intelligence and desire to join in a human partnership make them ideal candidates for intelligent aids to the handicapped.

Guide Dogs

A book dedicated to German Shepherd Dog training would hardly be complete without mentioning one of their most visible and admirable endeavors. "Blind-man's dogs" have been mentioned in history for several centuries. In the past, dogs employed as assistants for handicapped persons received no special selection or training. The blind or disabled person somewhat trained the dog. Those dogs were very different from the highly trained Assistance Dogs of today.

During the years following World War I, between 1917 and 1920, Germany began establishing specialized facilities to train guide dogs to assist veterans who had lost their sight in the war due to poisonous gas. German Shepherds were the primary dogs used in this work.

The late 1920s saw the beginning of a unique system of training guide or Seeing Eye dogs in the United States. The La Salle Kennels of German Shepherd Dogs was founded in 1926. From that kennel, the Master Eye Foundation of America was incorporated in Minneapolis, Minnesota. It is a nonprofit, nonsectarian institution. At about the same time, Josef Weber, a German Army war dog trainer, established another guide dog training facility.

History of American Guide Dogs

The guide dog movement in America really caught hold when a female German Shepherd named Kiss Fortunate Fields was brought to New Jersey by a sightless young man who refused to be constrained by his handicap. Her new master quickly changed the dog's name to Buddy.

This outstanding dog came from a German Shepherd training kennel located in Vevey, Switzerland. Fortunate Fields was the name of the kennel, which, in 1924, was in the business of producing "super dogs." Mrs. Harrison Eustis, an American from Pennsylvania, owned the kennel.

Buddy's blind owner was Mr. Morris Frank, a businessman from Nashville, Tennessee. He was alerted to the existence of guide dogs in 1927 through an article published in the *Saturday Evening Post,* written by Mrs. Eustis. In the article, Mrs. Eustis extolled the virtues of guide dogs in common use in Germany at the time.

Mr. Frank corresponded with Mrs. Eustis, and journeyed to Fortunate Fields, where he contracted with Mrs. Eustis for Buddy's services. For many years, Buddy and Morris were a common sight on the streets of Nashville, and their visibility inspired more sightless people to follow in their footsteps.

In 1929 Mrs. Harrison Eustis and Morris Frank planned and inaugurated The Seeing Eye, an American training facility dedicated to the training of guide dogs. Elliot Humphrey and Willi Ebeling were involved with this successful project and Mr. Weber was one of the first trainers. The Seeing Eye began operation in Nashville, and was later moved to Morristown, New Jersey.

The Seeing Eye

To quote from a brochure published by The Seeing Eye guide dog institution: "The Seeing Eye is more than a place. It is a philosophy, a program and a metaphor for independence."

This institution has bred and trained many thousands of dogs, using hundreds of expert trainers who are dedicated to helping the blind. Seeing Eye dogs have changed the lives of thousands of graduates, many of whom would otherwise be limited in their mobility. Guide dogs add another dimension to the scope of an otherwise accomplished individual, and allow that individual to live a more pleasant, functional life.

Traits. The most important trait of a guide dog is inherent intelligence. The dog also must have a particularly stable personality, and not be easily upset. Guide dogs must necessarily be large and strong enough for long hours of work, yet they can't be aggressive and must keep the welfare of their masters foremost in their minds. They must be willing to perform feats the average companion dog would never do, and do this for no wages except the approval and praise of their owner. In short, the ability of a guide dog is phenomenal, and the techniques used in training them are inspired.

Training. Guide dogs aren't only trained to use an instinctive faculty they already posses, as are tracking dogs, nor are their natural searching instincts expanded upon, as is the case with bird dogs. They aren't asked to kill game for their masters, an expansion of another inherent trait present in almost all descendants of the wolf, nor are they asked to attack their master's enemies as guard dogs.

The Seeing Eye Inc. is the oldest existing guide dog school in the world. It has hundreds of dogs in training year-round. The institution breeds its own German Shepherds, Labrador Retrievers, and Golden Retrievers. Occasionally, the institution provides Boxers to students who are allergic to long-haired dogs. Dams and sires of the gene pool are selected for trainability, health, and temperament.

Between the ages of 2 months and 18 months, a puppy is placed in the home of a volunteer puppy raiser, where it is taught basic obedience and socialization and is given lots of love.

Here is a dog taught to dedicate his life to his sightless partner. In doing so, he is called upon daily to make quick decisions and judgment calls of his own, based on his intelligence, cumulative experience, training, and knowledge. He must be cognizant of heights, distances, speeds, and other unlikely factors with which a blind person is faced. He must instantly refuse his master should he be commanded to perform some task that will endanger his human partner (intelligent disobedience, see page 160).

He must be able to accept every new distraction without special training or conditioning. Other animals, airplanes, fast moving automobile traffic, boats, and buses are taken in stride. He must work every minute his harness is in place, and sometimes when it is not. He must never let a new and different challenge perplex his train of thought.

Judging a dog's ability. Intelligence tests in learning and problem-solving ability are used to predict which dogs can best learn the complex tasks associated with guiding the blind. To be a good guide dog, a dog must also have a particular type of personality allowing the dog to achieve a useful level of functioning. Personality or temperament is, in part, genetically determined, and partly a result of handling and training.

I once read of a German Shepherd guide dog that was sleeping beside her master's hotel bed when a fire broke out in a room at the other end of the hallway. Long before the alarm sounded, the dog's sensitive nose detected smoke. The dog woke her master, took his hand in her mouth and led him down the stairs to safety well ahead of the crowd, demonstrating once more the dog's reasoning ability.

Guide Dogs for the Blind, Inc.

At Guide Dogs for the Blind, Labrador Retrievers (not Shepherds) are said to have the most success worldwide as guides. Those purebred Labs constitute the largest percentage of the breeding colony. They also have a small percentage of Golden Retrievers and breed Labrador-Golden crosses for use in their training program. The vast majority of trained dogs are bred from their own specially

selected stock. (Some say that Shepherds have fallen from favor because they bond so tightly with their first owners.)

Training

At about 18 months, the pup enters a four-month course of training at the institution, under sighted instructors. These instructors are carefully trained on site, and must complete three years of apprenticeship with ten dogs at a time. Rewards and corrections, consisting of verbal reprimands and loving tenderness, are used for this training.

As in much of the training mentioned in this book, each dog is taught basic obedience commands and to pull in harness. The training progresses to include work in heavy traffic and, interestingly, "intelligent disobedience." This term means the dog must use its discernment and experience to tell it whether or not to obey its sightless master. To teach a dog to use its own initiative and judgment must be the sublime aspect of training.

After four months of intensive training, a guide dog is ready for final exams with its instructor, who dares traffic of all types while wearing a blindfold.

Relinquishing Your Puppy

To raise a puppy for a guide dog facility is one way to enjoy a fine, purebred puppy at no significant cost to you or your family. The puppy lives with you, and the facility furnishes its vaccinations, health checkups, and spaying or neutering. You are obligated to housebreak the pup, train it to obey simple obedience commands, and inculcate its social graces.

There's only one problem: You must give up the dog when it is 16 to 18 months old. Perhaps you can obtain another to take its place, but somehow it isn't the same as having your own dog. Or is it? Just think of the satisfaction you receive from starting such a puppy's training, teaching a dog to fit into a life of service of the highest order.

Another aspect of working with a guide dog institution is the possibility of the institution having a retired dog to give away. These older dogs aren't all worn out, they are just beyond the age of usefulness to sightless people. They may have developed cataracts, or other age-related diseases, but they will have several more years as a companion.

Deaf Assistance

Dogs have a well-developed sense of hearing, nearly as acute as their sense of smell; they instinctively respond to sounds. Deaf assistance programs channel the dog's sound response to cause their owners to become physically aware of important sounds they are unable to hear. These assistance dogs alert their owners to various sounds by leading the person to the source of the sound, or by otherwise pointing out the sound.

This discipline was begun in 1976 by the American Humane Association, and has been carried forward by numerous American nonprofit organizations. It is an extremely valuable program in which many

German Shepherd Dogs, as well as other breeds, have been successfully trained.

In the program, dogs are specially trained to assist people with hearing loss by alerting them to important everyday sounds. These dogs are invaluable companions to the hearing impaired, and call their attention to ringing telephones, alarm clocks, doorbells, disturbances, crying babies, cooking timers, smoke alarms, and various other auditory warning signals.

The three or four months of specialized training begins when the dog is about a year old, and includes basic obedience as well as the need to physically warn owners of sounds they cannot hear.

Disability Dogs

Another discipline, or profession, in which dogs are trained is assisting the disabled. Amputees and other incapacitated people, such as stroke victims and heart patients, are assisted by these dogs. German Shepherds and other intelligent, easily trained breeds are taught to fetch newspapers, magazines, books, and other miscellaneous items for their owners. They are in constant attendance on their owners, and provide an invaluable service as well as companionship.

If a bedridden or wheelchair-bound person drops a comb, TV remote, or any other small item, the dog immediately picks it up and gives it to her owner. If the disabled person needs a box of tissues or a handkerchief, the dog fetches it, recognizing the item by its name.

In this capacity, the dog acts as a long arm for the disabled person. An assistance dog acts to minimize the work of the disabled person. It must learn an extensive vocabulary to be able to recognize by name such things as slippers, stockings, glasses, hat, coat, and various other needed items. If the disabled person tumbles from bed or a wheelchair, the dog is sometimes trained to bark or otherwise raise an alarm to call attention to her helpless master. Dogs trained in assistance work must, like guide dogs, have their master's welfare uppermost in mind.

In addition to the meaningful and useful traits described above is another less visible but highly significant value: companionship. The disabled person who has an assistance dog is often a person living alone or who is alone a great deal of the time. Such a person relates to the dog, loves it as family. The dog is more than a servant; it is a well-loved companion. The handicapped and their dogs form teams of two, each bringing happiness and love to the other, each finding happiness and fulfillment in their alliance.

16 Specialized Training

German Shepherd Dogs are among several working breeds that have been used in diverse ways in history. Shepherds filled many capacities in commerce and were often used as draft animals.

Carting

Carting is not a task generally associated with German Shepherds but many of these intelligent and willing dogs are trained to pull carts. The draft breeds usually used for this endeavor are the Bernese Mountain Dog, Saint Bernard, Bouvier des Flandres, Rottweiller, and Newfoundland. The Collie, Mastiff, and German Shepherd Dog are also commonly seen in informal draft exhibitions.

In this event, dogs are judged on their obedience to their handlers, their willingness to pull carts, and their desire to please their owners. Sometimes, it seems as if they are also judged on the style and polish of their equipment and trappings.

The maneuvers usually asked of the dogs are to pull a light cart at a normal speed and a slow speed, and to halt on command. They must be able to back, circle, make right-angle turns, and stay (wait) while the handler is absent. Normally, the dogs work on a leash, wearing a draft harness, which is a specially built padded piece of equipment, custom-fitted to the dog. The cart is usually a two-wheeled, lightweight wagon with shafts between which the dog stands. Four-wheeled wagons are also occasionally used, but they are more difficult to maneuver, nearly impossible to back, and may easily be overloaded.

The load in the light cart is balanced so as to distribute the weight squarely over the wheels; the dog therefore carries very little of the weight of the cart or its load.

In parades, a small child may ride in the cart, and if it is pulled on pavement or sidewalks, such duties should be no problem for a strong, healthy German Shepherd.

Because dogs aren't fully mature until about two years old, it is not recommended that carting be pursued before this age. It is further recommended that Duke receive a modicum of obedience training before he's hitched up, and when he's in harness he should be kept on a leash.

Weight-pulling Contests

These contests have been around for a very long time. They are held under similar rules by various organizations. The International Weight Pull Association (see page 183 for address and website) has members in many states and holds competitions on

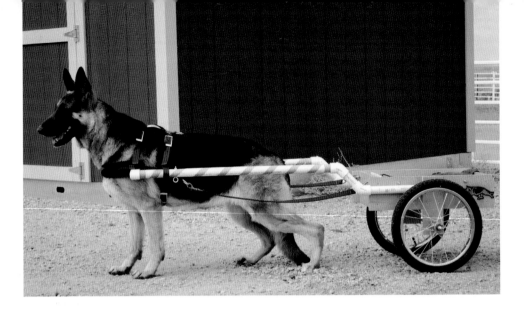

both snow and dry ground. Certificates and titles are awarded to winning dogs competing in each weight class.

Usually, the requirement is for a dog to pull a weighted sled a distance of 16 feet (4.9 m) in no more than 60 seconds. Dogs usually seen participating in these contests are Newfoundlands, Saint Bernards, Alaskan Malamutes, Siberian Huskies, Samoyeds, and other northern breeds.

An occasional German Shepherd is seen in such contests, which are judged in various weight classes. Since the Shepherd is a strong, well-built dog of a weight that usually competes against the smaller draft breeds, it often turns in an amazingly fine performance.

Principal Attributes

Great strength should be the principal attribute of an entrant in a weight-pulling contest; however contests are often won by the most willing dogs, the ones with the greatest desire to please their masters.

This is usually a contest to demonstrate which dog in a given weight range is in the best athletic condition, is the best muscled, and has been trained to pull properly. Conditioning and training are of utmost importance!

Equipment

As in draft work, pulling dogs must be fitted with proper weight-pulling harnesses. Shepherds under two years old or with any health problem should not be entered, even though rules usually allow all dogs over one year old to enter.

Procedure

1. In pulling tests, Duke's harness is hitched to either a sled or a wagon loaded with carefully weighed cement blocks. A measured length of string is attached to a rear corner of the wagon. The 16-foot (4.9-m) string has a small peg attached to the free end. The peg

Home Schooling

When Duke is three or four months old, buy a pulling harness and begin hitching him to weights about twice or three times a week. The pulling harness has tugs or traces that ride low along his rib cage to distribute the weight evenly. The tugs are fitted with a wooden "spreader bar" that acts to hold the tugs apart and prevent rubbing on his legs.

Let him drag small tires, lightweight logs, and other things in the yard, but don't press him to pull heavier weights. The objects should always be light enough for him to handle without undue stress. Give him rewards of petting and praise each time he pulls the weight. Never try to train him by hitching him to a tree or other immovable object with his pulling harness. Dogs don't understand isotonic exercise, and may injure themselves. If he enjoys pulling, and looks forward to this training, you can continue.

If Duke is reluctant to pull even the lightest burdens, and instead lies down or sits, don't fret. You can revert to lighter objects, but don't browbeat him. Some Shepherds seem to reason that these contests are only feats of strength, and they don't want to waste their intelligence on such endeavors. There is no reason to force Duke to continue training if he doesn't like it. Instead, you should move to other lessons requiring athletic ability instead of brute strength.

If you decide to move ahead, take Duke to your veterinarian before you begin heavy training. Have him examined and evaluated for hip dysplasia and other hereditary conditions that might be aggravated by weight training or may interfere with his ability or desire to pull. The veterinarian may advise you not to begin training until after his second birthday. After Duke's hips have been X-rayed, and he is proven to be free of signs of hip dysplasia is the best time to start heavy weight training.

Remember: Muscle development must be gained slowly. During the training period, feed the dog the best ration you can buy. If you are unsure, ask your veterinarian to recommend a working diet and possibly a supplement to promote muscle development. This diet, of course, can be started long before weight training is begun.

is inserted into the ground or snow beside the corner of the sled or wagon.

2. The handler leads Duke forward until the harness traces are tight. She then moves several feet in front of the dog and uses whatever command she desires to initiate pulling: She can coax him, slap the ground, or urge her dog on vocally. Any technique may be used except touching the dog or using food to entice him.

3. As the sled moves forward, the 16-foot (4.9-m) string tightens, and the peg pops out of the ground. Duke is then rested until all dogs in his weight class have attempted to move the sled. Additional weight is added to the sled, and the entire process is repeated. When one dog is able to move the weight, and no others can duplicate his efforts, he is declared the winner.

Virtually every large breed is occasionally entered in these contests. Sometimes a smaller dog in exceptional physical condition and with a big heart wins. He has learned how to plant his feet to exert the necessary pressure and start the load moving and is dedicated to performing whatever task his owner asks of him.

These fun contests are often a part of fairs and various other gatherings. In the winter, they are often staged on packed snow, where a sled is used to carry the weights. In summer, the weights are stacked on rubber-wheeled wagons placed on smooth packed ground on which the dog's footing is solid.

Frisbee Contests

[Frisbee is the registered trademark of Wham-O, Inc., U.S. No. 679,186, issued May 26, 1959 for toy flying saucers used for toss games.]

This is a sporting event enjoyed by many human-canine teams. You and your German Shepherd can play Frisbee almost anytime and anywhere you desire. Before training begins, you should take Duke to your veterinarian for an examination to be sure he is physically sound. Playing Frisbee is a great way to give yourself and your dog needed exercise, but it requires stamina, athletic ability, and healthy bodies for both team members.

History

It all began in 1947 when Walter F. Morrison carved a flying disk from plastic. The disk underwent various design changes until 1955, when Wham-O Company purchased the production rights. In 1957 Wham-O began manufacturing the tossing toy, and in 1959 Wham-O was issued a registered trademark on the word *Frisbee*.

The first Frisbee was undoubtedly tossed from human hand to human hand, but within a short time, an enterprising canine jumped into the picture and intercepted the flying disk. From that time on, people have been playing Frisbee with their dogs.

It isn't a sport for every dog, but canine athletes have excelled in this endeavor as in no other. We would be remiss if we didn't identify the legendary Ashley Whippet, a purebred Whippet belonging to Alex Stein of Cleveland, Ohio. Ashley, sensing a Hollywood career, learned to jump, whirl, and twist acrobatically in the air as he caught the disks.

The dog and his master gave an outstanding demonstration, performing without permission between innings in a Dodger baseball game, for which Mr. Stein was arrested and during which Ashley was temporarily lost. Thereafter, they and their followers took their newfound sport to national television, White House performances, and the Super Bowl.

What Frisbee Tests

This sport tests your Shepherd's agility, leaping ability, and precision in timing catches. His performance depends on his desire to please, his response to applause, and his eye for spectacular catches.

Some dogs in *Freeflight* competition are trained to jump over the handler's back to make a catch; others catch two disks at one time. Some pivot and twist as they make sensational catches high in the air. They often play to the audience and seem to dote on approval.

Training and Equipment

Before Duke is introduced to the Frisbee, you should train yourself to consistently toss the disk. Your competency in throwing the Frisbee will be reflected in Duke's ability to catch it under any circumstance. Practice with friends and neighbors until your throwing is competent. To prevent injuries, don't allow Duke to play the game with throwers who don't understand the basics of disk throwing.

The toy used in Friskies Canine Frisbee Championship contests is called the Fastback Frisbee Disk. It weighs about 4 ounces (112 g) and is 9.25 inches (23 cm)

in diameter, and comes in various colors. The color of the disk is important once the arena of play is identified. As you can imagine, the competing dog must visualize his target plainly in order to make a spectacular catch. A smaller version can be obtained for younger, inexperienced dogs. When you buy a disk for training or competition, stay with smooth, flexible disks made from nontoxic plastic. When the disks become chewed and rough, either discard them or file the edges smooth to prevent abrasions of the dog's mouth.

Frisbee Competition

There are over 100 local competitions scattered over 40 states holding Frisbee "finals." This sporting activity is open to all dogs of all ages, purebred or not, and is a fun event for participants and competitors alike.

The competition consists of both *Throw and Catch* and *Freeflight*. Classes are separated to accommodate males and females.

Throw and Catch competitions are held using a circle with a diameter of 34 yards (31 m) and a 4-yard (3.7-m) square "thrower's box" in the center. Scoring is done by tracking the number of throws and catches completed in 90 seconds. The dog must catch the Frisbee and retrieve it to the box and his handler. When the dog catches the disk and lands inside the circle, he is awarded one point. Two points are awarded each time the dog lands outside the circle but touches the ground with one or more paws during the catch. Three points are awarded for each midair

catch when the dog lands outside the circle completely and no foot is touching the ground when the disk is caught.

Freeflight contests involve the handler throwing the disks from any location, and not waiting for the dog to retrieve the Frisbee. Again, the number of successful tosses and catches made in 90 seconds are counted. In this competition, style is important. Two or three judges award points from one to ten for each of three categories. Showmanship and execution, leaping ability, and degree of difficulty are each awarded points.

If dogs are entered in both Throw and Catch and Freeflight competition, they are given a total of 60 seconds in each category and their scores are added together.

This competition is not an AKC-sanctioned sport, but it is certainly a worthy one. Dogs must be well behaved and nonaggressive toward other competitors. They must be trained to focus their attention on the Frisbee and not be distracted by the audience or other dogs. An important feature of Frisbee competition training is to maintain control of your dog at all times. Be sure he doesn't rush in to participate before his turn is called.

These basic rules and others should be studied by any Frisbee competitor. As in all games, you can't expect to win if you don't understand the rules. Attend Frisbee contests; watch and talk with participants. Get permission to observe their training techniques for the fancy moves that win points. Your dog can master multiple catches and other superdog maneuvers if you and Duke are dedicated; being a bit of a ham doesn't hurt either.

Flyball

Flyball contests are timed to the exact second and are run as a relay involving four teams of about six dogs each. Like Agility, Flyball is a canine spectator sport that has become increasingly popular since the advent of electronic timers. Flyball competitions are nearly as exciting for the spectators as for the athletes and their owners. The Flyball course includes a 100-foot (30-m) straight track with jumps arranged across it. At one end of the track, a box is located and equipped with a foot lever that the participating dog steps on.

In a typical contest, the participating dog is given a signal and races full speed over four jumps that are placed in the path. Upon reaching the box, he immediately steps on the foot lever. A tennis ball is released from the box into the air. The contestant catches the ball, turns, and runs back down the path, over the jumps, and to his handler. The handler receives the ball and hands it to the next member of the team, who immediately rushes to the box, . . . , and so forth.

Competition is stiff. However, the height of the jumps is adjusted according to the height of the smallest dog of the team. Flyball is not an AKC-sanctioned event at this time, but Flyball proponents are found in nearly all states. It is strictly for fun but is becoming more standardized every year. Trophies are awarded. Team members are given points that, when added up, lead to titles that can be added to the dog's name. Dogs of various breeds are often found on one team. An energetic and speedy German Shepherd might find a place on a team.

Canine Freestyle

The World Canine Freestyle Organization defines this performance as follows, *"Musical Freestyle* is a choreographed musical program performed by handlers and their dogs. The object of musical freestyle is to display the dog and handler in a creative, innovative, and original dance, using music and intricate movements to showcase teamwork, artistry, costuming, athleticism, and style in interpreting the theme of the music." The organization also writes, "Musical Canine Freestyle or just Canine Freestyle is simply dancing with dogs to music. It is a fun sport for the owners and dogs, and the audience . . . Based on basic obedience training, it adds other dimensions such as music, timing, costuming, routine development, showmanship."

Training is complex. However, if you have a very trainable and focused Shepherd that excels in obedience, you might have a winner. Performances are polished and beautiful. The dogs are trained to perfection. When a dog misses a beat, the human partner just smiles and the two continue their dance.

Schutzhund Trials

Schutzhund means "protection dog" in German. According to Captain von Stephanitz, the father of this breed, the German Shepherd Dog has a long history in protective work dating to the Bronze Age. The Shepherd was very adept in the role of guarding his family and their flocks from interlopers of various types. In those days, the Shepherd was primarily a herding animal with the strength and intelligence to fight off wolves and other predators. His occupation necessitated speed, toughness, endurance, cleverness, and agility.

Schutzhund training originated in Germany in the late 1800s or early 1900s, with the earliest known Schutzhund examinations given in 1920 in Germany. They were originally developed to evaluate breeding programs for the German Shepherd Dog. Schutzhund began in the 1950s in the United States near San Francisco, California. Training and trials have become increasingly popular since the 1970s, and presently more than 150 Schutzhund clubs are found in America.

Debate over Schutzhund Training

Obedience training and socialization are probably the first and foremost factors to be considered in Schutzhund training. The next is tracking, and the last is protection.

If these factors were faithfully observed, dog fanciers and others who sometimes denounce Schutzhund trials and tests would have less reason to censure this training. Indeed, the handlers, breeds involved, and the individual dogs receiving this training occasionally come under public scrutiny and condemnation. Many dog-training authorities have stated that any well-bonded dog will demonstrate protective qualities without attack training.

Law enforcement agencies, courts, dog organizations, and the media often enter into this debate when Schutzhund-trained dogs run amuck and cause irreparable damage to innocent victims who happen to come into contact with them. In almost every such case, the owner or handler of the dog involved is not in control of the dog.

Schutzhund training of the average German Shepherd companion dog is quite time-consuming, and may even be counterproductive. The Shepherd is a trustworthy breed with significant inherent defensive attitudes and abilities. Training a dog with those innate defensive traits to use his strength, cleverness, and agility to "attack" may lead to disaster. This may be averted if all factors of Schutzhund training are properly taught.

Having a dog that is trained to attack confers a tremendous responsibility upon his owner. Schutzhund dogs will attack only when they perceive a threat from a menacing person or when they are commanded to do so, but the word "threat" is often open to interpretation by the dog.

Improper Schutzhund Instruction

There is another factor to be mentioned. Many of the dogs incriminated as being untrustworthy and deadly have never received proper Schutzhund training; instead, they have been given unsuitable and dangerous instruction. They are dogs inappropriately maintained in a backyard or pen without supervision. Boredom alone can cause dogs to look for trouble, especially when two or more are kept together. Ownership of a dog of any breed carries with it the responsibility to

exercise and train it, more so in cases of the big, athletic canines.

Most Schutzhund clubs won't accept an unsound or mean dog or an owner who is not responsible for his dog's actions. Schutzhund trainers usually have good rapport with their dogs, maintain proper, balanced nutrition, keep them in prime physical condition, and give them plenty of exercise and work. Most competitors are in training themselves and handle their own dogs. Schutzhund dogs often hold Obedience and show titles as well.

Schutzhund trials include a predominance of German Shepherd Dogs. This is only natural when one considers that this breed was the original reason for these trials. The trials are open to virtually every breed, and in recent years, many Doberman Pinschers, Rottweilers, Staffordshire Terriers, Bouvier des Flandres, Giant Schnauzers, and dogs of some smaller breeds are commonly seen competing.

Schutzhund Training

Schutzhund trials are not sponsored or sanctioned by the AKC. For this and a number of other reasons, Schutzhund training is another discipline that will not be discussed in depth. Some of the requirements and information about trials are furnished for anyone who wants to know more about this training.

Guard dog training is highly individualized. As a sport, Schutzhund training is fairly well organized, and there are many Schutzhund clubs in the United States that hold trials for their members.

Each Schutzhund club has its own training program made available to handlers with dogs of a certain age, usually 14 months. It is felt that this type of training should be given only to dogs that have reached their full mental and physical maturity. Since many of the judges are German, often the handlers use German commands, although this is left purely to the individual handler's discretion.

There are three parts to each level of training and awards are given after satisfactory completion of each level. Judging is often rather arbitrary and varies from judge to judge. Some of the judges may test the dog's disposition, in addition to its performance. They have no compunction about failing any dog that shows timidity, shyness, aggression, or fear.

Tracking Phase

In the tracking part of this training, the dog must follow a tracklayer's track scent for a designated distance. The club sets the track age and number and type of turns included in each level. The club also determines the numbers of articles dropped to be identified by the dog. The dog works on a long tracking line or off lead, but in either case, the handler must follow 30 feet (9 m) or more behind the dog.

Obedience Phase

This part of Schutzhund training is quite similar to AKC obedience training with the exception of distractions. In Schutzhund trials, guns are fired and moving people simulate an entirely different type of distraction for the competing dogs. These dogs must also climb or otherwise scale a fence. Judging is done on the basis of ability and interest as well as performance.

Protection Phase

Simulated attacks are used in this phase of Schutzhund training. This is the part of the training that draws the most public criticism, even though it might not be the most difficult part of training. In this phase, a padded assistant is given the role of aggressor. He plays the part of a menacing intruder and makes no bones about it. He waves his arms, yells, and makes threatening gestures toward the dog and his handler. The dog responds by attacking and biting the assistant's padded arm and holding on.

The assistant strikes the dog with a bamboo or willow stick to test the animal's courage. If the dog dodges the blows, but doesn't give up the attack, and renews his fight in spite of the blows, he is rated higher. If the dog runs to his handler or fails to hold the assistant, he is down-rated.

Needless to say, striking a dog's hindquarters, sides, and withers with a stick doesn't set well with many dog fanciers, their organizations, and members. Advocates of Schutzhund training respond by stating that the dog will watch and bark, but not attack, if the person stands quite still. They further state that the dog is responding to a direct threat, and a properly trained dog will let go and return to his handler on voice command to do so.

The dog is trained to locate the adversary assistant who is hiding behind one of several blinds set up in the trial field. When this antagonist is found, the well-trained dog will stand his ground, growl, and bark, but must not attack or bite unless the adversary launches some combative attack upon the dog or handler. As the handler escorts the identified aggressor off the field, the dog is trained to follow watchfully from a certain distance behind.

Winning dogs in the various competitions are awarded a great variety of titles.

If you are interested, and wish to learn more about local Schutzhund trials, dates, and results, read *Dog Sports* magazine or *Schutzhund USA*, published by the United Schutzhund Clubs of America, the address for which is found on page 184 of this book.

Police Dogs

If you look in the Third College Edition of *Webster's New World Dictionary*, you will find *police dog*, with this definition: "a German Shepherd specially trained to assist police." The term "Schutzhund" is of comparatively recent origin. It is not even listed in the von Stephanitz book's index, but *police dog* is a term frequently used by the same author. Captain von Stephanitz wrote: "The Police dog is such a natural and obvious institution that it is nothing marvellous (sic)." He further states that this police dog naturally evolved from Bronze Age Shepherds, which were, no doubt, the first faithful comrades of night watchmen (policemen). He traces tracking dogs to ancient Greece and Egypt, and he emphatically proclaims that the German Shepherd Dog inaugurated the Police Dog Movement. He relates Shepherds to police duties when they guarded flocks, turned

rural policemen, and sometimes by rural postmen as guard dogs and companions. Customs authorities and foresters made use of these dogs as well. They were trained for guard duty, sniffing out contraband, tracking lawbreakers, and carrying messages from one station to another.

Modern police dogs include several different breeds, although none may be quite so well suited to the work as the German Shepherd. The training of these dogs is done through dedicated handlers who have access to professional trainers to guide them. The dogs are taught tracking techniques, drug and other contraband detection, firearms detection, as well as the more traditional attack, guard, and protect duties.

Police dogs are the product of a combination of Schutzhund training and various other specialized training techniques. The German Shepherd Dog used in police work is a valuable tool of his trainer and handler, and is sometimes a tried-and-true family member as well. For security reasons, most police dogs live in a kennel when not on duty, although many are retired to their handlers' homes after accepting de-programming training.

back trespassers, tracked thieves, and held them at bay, leaving nothing unnoticed.

The police dog movement he spoke of began in Germany, with at least 450 police stations using these dogs in 1910. The movement spread quickly to Belgium, Austria, Holland, France, Switzerland, Poland, and other European countries. The German government supported the use of Shepherds in police work and sponsored several training facilities. These trained dogs were extensively used by

Bomb and Weapon Detection

Dogs in this category are trained to sniff and identify forcite, a common product found in many bombs.

Burnt cordite is a chemical common to weapons, and dogs can be trained to detect this odor as well.

Training to seek and call their handler's attention to these scents is another specialized discipline of some police dogs.

Drug Detection Dogs

In this and other specialized work, the German Shepherd is trained to detect certain organic odors. Drugs such as marijuana, cocaine, and others that are sometimes smuggled into the United States are not easily detected when included in personal luggage. The state and federal drug enforcement agencies often use dogs' acute olfactory senses to identify these drugs by training the dogs to react in a special way when the odors are detected.

Example: While waiting for a plane in the middle of the night a couple of years ago, I watched a young German Shepherd being challenged by drug enforcement agents. The first agent we saw opened three vacant lockers at random, placed a small envelope in each, and locked them shut. About half an hour later, the second agent brought in the dog, who was told to search the lockers.

That amazing dog ran his nose up and down the bank of lockers like a vacuum cleaner. When he came across a planted drug-containing envelope, he dug at the locker door and whined until his handler opened the door and removed the envelope. After receiving his reward consisting of a quick "*Good boy*" and a scratch behind the ears, he continued until the entire bank had undergone his search and all three envelopes had been removed.

This type of drug sniffing is invaluable to customs agents and a real problem for drug traffickers. German Shepherds and other breeds with good noses are used in this discipline.

Example: Recently, when going through customs in Brussels, Belgium, I was surprised to meet a dog standing beside a customs guard. As I walked past, the dog did a cursory smell of my pockets, my bag, my wife's bag, and her purse, whereupon I spoke to him. My little speech seemed to stimulate his interest, causing him to go over my pockets and bag a second time. Satisfied, he then walked back to his handler, sat down, and waited for his next "customer." I remarked that I felt much better with a dog sniffing my bag from the outside than a custom's agent rifling through the inside.

Fruit and Vegetable Identification

Dogs like the German Shepherd have terrific noses, and are trained to identify virtually any type of odor. Once we were waiting for an inter-island flight in Honolulu, and we watched a Beagle as she did her work. Every bag coming into the customs area was sniffed and approved. Then, when the little dog began to whine and scratch at one bag, the official sent the bag and owner to another room to explain why the suitcase full of raw fruit was being brought into the state in violation of Hawaiian quarantine laws.

In both of these types of detection, the dog is trained to detect certain specific scents. The methods used to train those incredible dogs to detect particular odors is simply a continuation of the scent training described previously. Instead of searching for an object with a human odor, they are trained to search for objects that have a drug or fruity odor.

War Dog Training

War dogs are mentioned in histories of the Egyptian era circa 4000 B.C., and in many pieces of historical literature since. These priceless companions of the armies of early times received the same honors as their masters, and in defeat they shared a common grave with them. They were often given funerals or were referred to in the memorials of the soldiers at whose side they fought.

War dogs were used as messengers by Frederick the Great, and in Europe they were used as assistants to fighting forces as early as the eighteenth century.

Russia and England used dogs in World War I; Germany is said to have used over 30,000 war dogs. America borrowed trained dogs from England, France, and Belgium, most of which served as messengers and guards.

Physical Strength, Stamina, and Intelligence

The toughness of German Shepherds proved to be just what the Department of Defense ordered. They were able to carry fairly large packs, medical kits, guns, and other equipment for long distances. Moving in a natural, easy trot they covered miles with little effort. They went without sleep for extended periods and never complained to their superior officers. German Shepherds were used extensively throughout World War II, the Korean War, and the war in Vietnam, and are still a vital factor in the United States defense system.

As war dogs, Shepherds' intelligence is uncanny. Used as scouts, messengers, and equipment carriers, they moved quickly and quietly to and from the front lines. Sentry dogs provided their human counterparts with another means of detecting enemies by using their acute canine sense of smell. As ambulance dogs, they sniffed out wounded soldiers and carried medical packs; as bomb dogs, they detected and alerted soldiers to the presence of unexploded grenades.

In all these capacities and others, the easily trained Shepherds enabled more men to move into duties in other areas.

The K-9 Corps

The United States Armed Forces began its use of dogs in May 1942 with a contingent of nine dogs assigned to sentry duty. They were obtained by an organization known as "Dogs for Defense, Inc.," a nonprofit organization formed in New York City to serve as the government's procurement agency for dogs. This organization preceded the establishment of the K-9 Corps.

Thereafter, approximately 20,000 dogs were trained to help allied forces in every theater of conflict. During much of World War II, more than 1,500 dogs, many of which were German Shepherds, were inducted each month into the various branches of the armed services. Special trainers instructed men and dogs, who formed intimate teams excelling in every field of endeavor.

- These dogs received basic obedience training and were also taught to wear muzzles and gas masks. They were exposed to gunfire, aircraft, and small boat transportation during their 12 weeks of basic training.
- Dogs were trained to carry medical packs or first aid and surgical kits, giving valuable assistance to the medical staff.
- Ambulance or casualty dogs underwent specialized scent training enabling them to determine whether or not a wounded soldier was alive. When they discovered a live casualty on the battlefield, they barked or hurried to the medics to announce their discovery. This action alone saved thousands of lives in World War II.
- Sentry dogs worked with their military handlers and used their acute olfactory sense to assure that an enemy soldier waiting in ambush would never surprise them. These dogs were often trained to give silent alarms such as stopping, sitting, or raising their hackles. Sentry dogs and their handlers were commonly seen patroling military bases, sea installations, beaches, ammunition dumps, and vital defense locations. They were used to patrol perimeters of civilian factories and critical shipping depots as well.

- Scout dogs were similarly employed by the military to work off leash to seek and identify strangers. German Shepherds excelled in this work, since they seem to be able to scent different races as well as different individuals. Canine scouts move without noise, their soft pads and surefootedness adding secrecy to their many other qualifications.
- Shepherds and other war dogs were quickly trained to carry dispatches and important troop movement messages between posts, often behind enemy lines where no telephone communication was possible; they also carried phone lines to outposts.
- One of the chief uses of Shepherds in World War II was in land mine detection. These dogs' acute olfactory sense allowed them to point out any area where the soil was freshly disturbed, thus detecting mines long before they posed a risk to either a soldier or his dog.

177

The term "war dogs" is arbitrarily used for dogs serving in the armed forces of the United States. As a breed, the German Shepherd has distinguished itself in all conflicts with which the United States has been associated since World War I. Hundreds of photographs of American war dogs are available to illustrate the importance and significance of these dogs in past wars. Many of these photos confirm the predominance of German Shepherds in this field of endeavor.

In peacetime, these dogs are also invaluable to American soldiers, sailors, and coastguardsmen. They are regularly employed in sentry duty, drug detection, bomb detection, gun detection, and other specialized functions.

Disaster and Avalanche Search

Special training is given to German Shepherds and other scenting dogs used to locate victims of hurricanes, tornadoes, floods, snowslides, and other natural disasters. Unfortunately, these same dogs are sometimes needed to assist in searching for victims of bombings and other senseless destruction in the world. This training may include differentiation between living and deceased beings in addition to finding people in either category.

SARDUS

The Search and Rescue Dogs of the United States (SARDUS) is a volunteer organization made up of teams of dog handlers and their dogs. This organization offers the following training information.

If you wish to take up this fascinating and rewarding volunteer occupation, expect to spend at least 18 months in personal and rescue training for your dog. Dogs progress from air scent trailing to water search, avalanche search, then to disaster search.

A written certification of performance standard is awarded to dogs by the various organizations to which the teams belong. This certification must be given before dogs are used in actual search situations.

It is best to begin this specialized training with puppies eight weeks old, so as to avoid counterproductive behavior such as chasing wildlife.

Ms. Wichmann, treasurer for SARDUS, offers an interesting estimation. She guesses that less than 20 percent of the dog and handler teams beginning this work are successful. At the present time, she estimates there are 100 or fewer groups of Search and Rescue teams in existence in the United States. Each group consists of between one and 20 teams of dogs and their handlers.

Figures on Disaster Dogs are easier to calculate; the Federal Emergency Management Agency has written a national standard for Disaster Dogs. The agency has a record of 110 to 120 certified disaster teams as of this writing. German Shepherd Dogs, Labrador Retrievers, and Golden Retrievers are the breeds most commonly used in this work. Instinctive traits of herding, retrieving, and pleasing their masters are of utmost importance and will usually lead to successful Search and Rescue and Disaster Dog training.

Ms. Wichmann offers a learned opinion about the complexities of the training of these dogs. Airborne scent is easiest to learn and accomplish by most dogs. Water and avalanche detection is more difficult, and usually takes longer, more intensive training. Disaster search is the most advanced education of the three, requiring more training and practice.

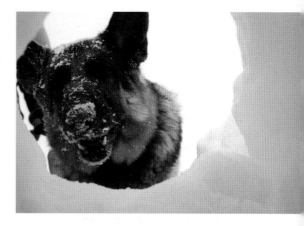

These dogs have been known to detect leaks in pipes buried in soil several feet below ground level. They can pick up minute concentrations of the gas and thus locate small, but dangerous and expensive, leaks. Scent dogs such as the German Shepherd have a proven ability to find and mark leaks undetectable by sophisticated modern machinery.

Pipeline Scenting

This specialized training is perhaps less intensive and certainly of another order. It is a commercial endeavor, one that is quite useful to the oil and gas industries. For this job, a German Shepherd is trained to identify the special odor of butyl mercaptans. Such dogs are generally in small demand, but under certain circumstances, these specialty dogs earn fabulous wages for doing something they enjoy. They may work miles of hidden pipeline per day, and save the hiring company many thousands of dollars with each leak they find.

Conclusion

Historically, German Shepherds have the desire, ability, and talent to do practically everything any dog has ever been trained to do. Your German Shepherd is no exception. The time you spend with your companion, learning and teaching, will be amply rewarded many times over. Use his time well, keep him busy and always on the leading edge of the learning curve, and he will be a happier animal. We have only scratched the surface, but hopefully we have shown you how to begin to train this marvelous animal.

Home Schooling

Frisbee Training

Dogs with long muzzles have an advantage in this sport. Duke should be a good choice for Frisbee training if he is physically sound, likes to play catch with a ball, and shows an interest in disks. If he has been taught to fetch, you should be able to predict his ability to catch a Frisbee. If he watches the dummy being tossed, marks it, and is anxious to retrieve it, he will probably appreciate Frisbee. Wait until he is about six months old before you begin training. This will allow his permanent teeth to be solidly in place before he tries catching the whirling flying disk.

The usual obedience lessons should be mastered prior to Frisbee training. As in other sports, good manners and quick responses to basic obedience commands are important to control Duke during his training period. It is critical that he knows "Come," and it will help if he has been taught "Fetch" and "Give."

Remember that this is a high-energy sport for the dog. His training and practice should be accomplished in cool weather. The turf on which he performs should also have safe footing and be conducive to jumping and making sliding landings. Stay away from asphalt, concrete, or gravel surfaces. Pick a park, a big backyard, pasture, or other large, grassy, relatively flat spot. The sand of a beach is often used, but may be a dangerous place to train or play Frisbee with your dog as broken bottles, sharp seashells, and jellyfish might pose a threat to Duke's footpads.

Familiarize Duke with the disk early in life. Put a Frisbee in his crate when he is being housetrained. Roll a disk for him to chase on the floor and encourage him to play with the toy. Once he begins to pay attention to the disk, and his interest seems to be increasing, put the Frisbee away and take it out only for playtime. As with his other toys, he will learn its name and will appreciate it more if it is kept as a special treat. Training sessions, as with other tasks, should occupy no more than five minutes at a time. This training can be interspersed with his other training, and should be repeated several times a day if possible.

Dogs can be made to react to a particular object, especially if it is used to tease them. The flapping burlap arm-wrapping of a Schutzhund instructor is used to teach a police dog to grab the padded arm of a "criminal" (see page 170 for Schutzhund discussion). In the same way, teasing Duke with a Frisbee can increase the interest of the pup.

1. Wave the disk gently in front of his face and encourage him to bite at it. When he grabs it, tug a bit, then cause him to release the disk by offering him a treat and commanding him "Give." In this way, you not only reward him for grabbing the disk, you also let him understand exactly what you want him to do.
2. After he is grabbing and releasing the disk on command, try tossing it a short distance. When he runs after it, he will probably pick it up and look around for you. Tell him "Come" and quickly back up while facing him and extending your

hand to him. He should bring it to you and receive his reward, including a great deal of praise. If he drops it instead, take him to it, pick up the disk, and cause him to grab it once more, then finish the exercise as before.

3. Within a few days, Duke should be routinely retrieving the Frisbee and receiving his reward from you. The next step is to toss it into the air in a sailing motion and encourage him to chase and catch it. A few *"Get the Frisbee, Duke"* commands will give him the idea. These early tosses of the disk should be no more than a few feet. Once he has mastered the task of

catching the Frisbee while it is airborne, he is on his way.

As in retrieving, there is no excuse for him to take the Frisbee and run in the opposite direction with it. Insist that he bring the disk to you and put it into your hand. If need be, you can use a long check line on his collar to enforce this part of training. If he already has mastered *"Come"* and *"Give,"* it should be natural to him to make the connection. In a way, this is an advanced type of retrieving.

It seems likely that there should be Frisbee training classes in existence, but at this time, none are known.

Useful Addresses and Literature

Books

Abbott, Brenda E., Executive Editor. *The German Shepherd Book*. Wheatridge, CO: Hoflin Publishing Ltd., 1986.

Beaver, Bonnie V. *Canine Behavior*. Philadelphia, PA: W. B. Saunders Co., 1999.

Brown, Beth. *Dogs That Work for a Living*. New York: Funk & Wagnalls, 1970.

Bryson, Sandy. *Search and Rescue Dog Training*. Pacific Grove, CA: Boxwood Press, 1976.

Burnham, Patricia G. *Playtraining Your Dog*. New York: St. Martin's Press, 1980.

Colflesh, Linda. *Making Friends*. New York: Howell Book House, 1990.

Coren, Stanley. *The Intelligence of Dogs*. New York: The Free Press, Division of MacMillan, Inc., 1994.

Davis, Henry P. *The Modern Dog Encyclopedia*. Harrisburg, PA: The Stackpole Co., 1958.

Dodge, Geraldine and Josephine Rine. *The German Shepherd Dog in America*. New York: Orange Judd Publishing Co., 1956.

Hartwell, Dickson. *Dogs Against Darkness*. New York: Dodd Mead & Co., 1942.

Hebard, Caroline. *So That Others May Live*. New York: Bantam Books, 1995.

Johnson, Glen R. *The Companion Dog*. New York: Howell Book House, 1991.

Johnson, Glen R. *Tracking Dog, Theories and Methods*. Canastota, NY: Arner Publications, Inc., 1975.

Lithgow, Scott. *Training and Working Dogs*. St. Lucia, Queensland, Australia: University of Queensland Press, 1987.

McDonnell, Virginia B. *Foster Pups*. Camden, NJ: Thomas Nelson & Sons, 1966.

Ogden, Paul. *Chelsea, the Story of a Signal Dog*. New York: Little Brown and Co., 1992.

Pearsall, Margaret E. *The Pearsall Guide to Successful Dog Training*. New York: Howell Book House, 1980.

Pearsall, Milo and Hugo Verbruggen. *Scent*. Loveland, CO: Alpine Publications, Inc., 1982.

Putnam, Peter Brock. *Love in the Lead*. New York: E.P. Dutton, 1979.

Saunders, Blanche. *Complete Book of Dog Obedience*. New York: Howell Book House, 1969.

Simmons-Moake, Jane. *Agility Training*. New York: Howell Book House, 1991.

Syrotuck, William G. *Scent and the Scenting Dog*. Canastota, NY: Arner Publications, Inc.,1972.

Von Stephanitz, Max. *The German Shepherd Dog in Word and Picture* (American Edition). Wheat Ridge, CO: Donald R. Hofling, 1995.

Organizations

American Association of Working
Trial Societies
c/o Mark Donnell
800 Wagon Wheel Trail
Georgetown, TX 78628
http://waggin-tails.com/workingtrials

American Kennel Club (AKC)
5580 Centerview Drive, Suite 200
Raleigh, NC 27606-3390
(919) 233-9767
www.akc.org

Assistance Dogs International
Shiela O'Brien
NEADS
P.O. Box 213
W. Boylston, MA 01583
www.assistancedogsinternational.org

Cycle Ashley Whippet Invitational
Box 725
Encino, CA 91426
www.ashleywhippet.info/history.html

Delta Society
875 124th Avenue NE, Suite 101
Bellevue, WA 98005

German Shepherd Dog Club of America
Blanche Beisswenger
17 W. Ivy Lane
Englewood, NJ 07631
www.gsdca.org

German Shepherd Dog Club of Canada
Christine Gibbons
Rockwood, ONT Canada NOB 2K0
www.gsdcc.ca.org

German Shepherd Dog Rescue
Diane Reppy
P.O. Box 117
New Ringold, PA 17960
www.gsdrescue.org

Guide Dog Foundation for the Blind
Peggy Teufel
371 Jericho Turnpike
Smithtown, NY 11787-9897
www.guidedog.org

Guide Dogs for the Blind
P.O. Box 151200
San Rafael, CA 94915
www.guidedogs.org

Guiding Eyes for the Blind
611 Granite Springs Road
Yorktown Heights, NY 10598
www.guideingeyes-md.org

Institute for Canine Massage
P.O. Box 2786
Loveland, CO 80539
www.dogmassage.com

International Search and Rescue
Trade Association
David Rider
4537 Foxhall Drive NE
Olympia, WA 98506
http://rescueinternational.org

International Weight Pull Association
3455 Railroad Avenue
Post Falls, ID 83848
www.iwpa.net

National Association for SAR
P.O. Box 3709
Fairfax, VA 22038
www.nasar.org/nasar/specialty_fields.php

National Association of Dog
Obedience Instructors
2286 East Steele Road
St. Johns, MI 48879
www.nadoi.org

North American Search Dog Network
Joyce Phares
RR2 Box 32
Urbana, IL 61801
www.nasdn.org

Owners Handlers Association of America
RD 1, Box 755
Millerstown, PA 17602
www.canineworld.com/oha

SAR Dogs of the United States
P.O. Box 11411
Denver, CO 80211
www.sardogsus.org

Seeing Eye
P.O. Box 375
Morristown, NJ 07963-0375
www.seeingeye.org

Support Dogs, Inc.
11645 Lilburn Park Road
St. Louis, MO 63146
www.supportdogs.org

United Schutzhund Clubs of America
3704 Lemoy Ferry Road
St. Louis, MO 63125
www.germanshepherddog.com

United States Dog Agility Association
P.O. Box 850955
Richardson, TX 75085-0955
www.usdaa.com

Periodicals

AKC Gazette
5580 Centerview Drive, Suite 200
Raleigh, NC 27606-3390
(919) 233-9767
www.akc.org/pubs/gazette

Dog Sports Magazine
DSM Publishing, Inc.
940 Tyler Street, Studio 17
Benicia, CA 94510-2916
www.dogsports.com

Dog World
29 North Wacker Drive
Chicago, IL 60606
www.dogworldmag.com

Front & Finish (Obedience Magazine)
P.O. Box 333
Galesburg, IL 61402
www.frontandfinish.com

German Shepherd Quarterly
Hoflin Publications Ltd.
4401 Zephyr Street
Wheat Ridge, CO 80033-3299
*www.hoflin.com/magazines/
magazines.html*

Schutzhund USA
3704 Lemay Ferry Road
St. Louis, MO 63125
*www.germanshepherddog.com/
usa_magazine.htm*

Therapy Dogs International
Ann Lettis
91 Wiman Avenue
Staten Island, NY 10308
www.tdi_dog.org

Glossary

A-frame: Agility trial obstacle over which dog must climb.

Agility trial: Timed sporting event in which dogs must master a group of obstacles laid out in a course.

Agrarians: Tillers of the soil; farmers.

Airborne scent: Body odor swept from an animal's body and carried by air currents.

Alpha dog: Leader of the pack; chief dog.

Ambulance dogs: K-9 corps dogs given the responsibility for finding live casualties on the battlefield.

Aptitude: Natural ability or talent; general suitability.

Associative learning: Method of teaching a dog by linking an act to a reward.

Avalanche dogs: Rescue dogs trained to find people trapped under snow.

Backyard breeder: Amateur or hobby producers of dogs, not necessarily interested in improving the breed.

Balance point: In herding, the point at which a dog has the most influence on the livestock.

Biddable: Cooperative dog, willing to obey handler.

Bite: Position of dog's incisor teeth when mouth is closed.

Body language: Physical attitude of a dog that tells handler what action dog is considering.

Bond: Invisible reciprocal attachment between a dog and its master.

Bumper: A stuffed canvas retrieving toy that resembles a boat fender.

Burnt cordite: Explosive powder that dogs are taught to scent.

Canidae: Canine family that includes dogs, wolves, coyotes.

Canis familiaris: Genus and species of domestic dog.

Carnivore: An animal that subsists primarily on animal flesh.

Cast: Send forth a herding, scenting, or hunting dog.

Champion: Dog that has competed in AKC shows or trials and earned sufficient points to be awarded Champion title.

CHD: Canine Hip Dysplasia; a hereditary deformity of femur and pelvis.

Check-cord/check-line: Long, lightweight line attached to dog's collar to enable handler to control dog from a distance.

Choke collar: Chain or nylon check collar used for training.

Cognitive ability: Capacity to understand or absorb knowledge.

Conformation: Form and structure of dog compared to breed standard.

Congenital disease: Deformity present at birth, not necessarily hereditary.

Contact obstacles: Agility term referring to items that must be climbed or walked upon rather than being jumped over.

Crate training: Teaching dog to go to and stay in an enclosure.

Cross-over: Agility term referring to an object the dog must climb and descend from designated sides.

Cryptorchid: Dog with both testicles retained in abdominal cavity.

Dead ring: On training collar, the ring through which the chain is dropped to form a noose.

Dependence: Trust in and reliance of a dog on its handler.

Direct negative reinforcement: Physical correction of a dog using a personal disciplinary measure such as scolding or hitting.

Discipline: 1. Training in specific endeavor. 2. Chastisement or punishment. 3. Control.

DNA: Deoxyribonucleic acid, a molecular basis of heredity, located in tissue cells nuclei.

Dog show: Judged canine exhibition used to compare registered dogs to the breed standard and to each other.

Dog walk: Agility obstacle consisting of an elevated plank over which the contestant must walk from end to end.

Dominance training: Activities for owners to use to establish themselves as dominant members of a dog's pack.

Draft: Dogs used to pull carts or weights.

Drive: 1. Evidence of power of dog in performance. 2. In herding, the movement of a herd away from handler.

Elbow dysplasia: Ununited anconeal process; hereditary, developmental deformity of elbow joint.

Fecal exam: Microscopic examination of feces for evidence of parasite ova.

Feral: Wild; undomesticated, or having escaped from domestication.

Fetch: Game in which handler throws an article, which is recovered and returned by dog.

Find: Command telling dog to locate a specific scented object or person.

Focus: Concentration of dog upon handler.

Force: To physically cause dog to do something beyond its natural inclination. Restraint and dominance training are types of force. Force does not imply abuse.

Forcite: Chemical substance common to many bombs, which dogs are trained to identify.

Freeflight: A judged Frisbee event.

Fringe following: Action of dogs that pursue airborne scents as opposed to track scents.

Frisbee: 1. A plastic disk manufactured for throwing and catching. 2. A judged canine competition using disks.

Gene pool: Collection of genes of all dogs in the breeding population.

Gripping: Grasping or biting and hanging onto herded animals by dog.

Habituation: Training by becoming accustomed or conditioned to a given incident or situation.

Heartworm: Blood stream parasite of dogs, spread by mosquitoes.

Herbivorous: Creatures who derive nutrition solely from plants.

Herding: 1. AKC group of dogs. 2. Dogs trained to surround, collect, and move other animals at signal of handler.

Herding instinct: Natural or inherent ability to collect and move other animals.

Hereditary: Genetically transmitted.

Hovawart: Ancient and modern German dog breed, possibly included in German Shepherd Dog ancestry.

Hyperactive: Dog displaying excessive activity with attention deficit.

Imprinting: Rapid learning process that takes place early in the life of a social animal and establishes a behavior pattern.

Innate: Inherent; natural; factors that are present from birth.

Instinct: A natural or inherent aptitude.

Intelligence: The ability to learn, understand, and solve problems through reasoning.

Intelligent disobedience: The inherent ability of a guide dog to use its discernment and experience to decide whether or not to obey its sightless master.

Legitimate breeder: One whose primary interest is bettering the breed.

Lift: Herding term relating movement of livestock toward handler.

Linetracker: Dog that has the desired tracking behavior.

Mis-marked: Coat with markings that are undesirable for conformation showing.

Monorchid: Having one testicle retained in abdominal cavity.

Mouthing: Normal action of a puppy investigating its environment by tasting.

Multiple-iaid track: Heavily established track scent laid by repeatedly traversing the track.

Negative reinforcement: Dissuading a dog from repeating an incorrect response to training by scolding or physically correcting the behavior.

Neophobia: Fear of new things. Dominant characteristic of feral animals that is undesirable in training prospects.

Neoteny: Immature characteristics retained in adulthood.

Nest etiquette: Manners governing young puppies' actions in presence of dam and siblings.

Nose: Dog's ability to scent.

Obedience: Discipline involving modification of many different behaviors through extensive training.

OFA: Orthopedic Foundation for Animals, the organization that reads and evaluates X-rays for hereditary diseases.

Olfactory sense: Ability to smell and differentiate odors.

Olfactory system: Organs and tissues associated with smell.

Outrun: Cast; move of a herding dog away from handler to balance point.

Overbreeding: Promiscuous breeding; breeding of poor quality bitches because of popularity of breed.

Overshot: Upper incisors that protrude over lowers.

Pack mentality: Innate wolflike instinct of dog to be loyal to the pack leader, either canine or human.

Pause table: Agility obstacle consisting of raised platform on which the contestant stops, lies down, and pauses.

Pedigree: Genealogical chart of a dog showing a few generations of ancestors.

Penning: Driving livestock into a pen.

Personality tests: Evaluation of weanling puppies by trained individuals to provide a guide for training prospects.

Pet-quality: Purebred dog that has features that make it undesirable for conformation showing or breeding.

Pheromone: Chemical produced by animals that stimulates a behavioral response by others.

Positive reinforcement: Any reward for proper performance.

Possessive personality: Dog's recognition of its responsibility to its master. A very desirable trait in training prospects.

Progenitor: Ancestor or parent.

Progeny: Offspring or descendents.

Prong collar: Restraint device using a series of blunt prongs that turn into dog's neck when tightened.

Punishment: Physical negative reinforcement of a command.

Puppy mill/puppy factory: Dog-breeding establishment that places quantity above quality of puppies produced.

Quarter: Moving back and forth in front of handler to catch a scent.

Release: The final phase of training a specific task; command that returns the dog to its normal status.

Remote reinforcement: Use of a separated or distant tool to assist in training. Squirt bottle, long line, noise.

Retractile lead: Long leash contained within a spring-loaded handle that can be drawn in quickly.

Reward: Any recognized appreciation given to dog being trained.

Schutzhund: Specially trained protection dog.

Scout dogs: Members of K-9 corps specially trained to seek and identify strangers.

Search and rescue dogs: Those specially trained to seek lost or injured humans, and to assist in their recovery.

Seesaw: Agility obstacle over which dog must walk.

Selective breeding: Scientific mating to encourage or produce specific characteristics in offspring.

Sentry dogs: K-9 corps dogs trained to patrol perimeters of military establishments to call attention to interlopers.

Show-quality: Registered dogs having excellent conformation, color, and movement according to breed standard.

Siblings: Littermates; brothers and sisters.

Single track: Scent track made by one trip.

Socialization: Process of adapting to a human environment.

Stack: Trained stance taken by show dog for judging.

Steptracking: Concentrated body movement taken by serious trackers.

Submissive/subservient attitude: Combination of postures taken by a puppy when meeting other dogs.

Survival instinct: Innate desire to find food, shelter, and to procreate the species.

Temperament: Personality; mental attitude or character of a dog.

Thrower's box: In Frisbee contests, the designated spot for the handler to stand.

Tidbits: Physical rewards or food.

Tire jump: Agility obstacle consisting of a suspended automobile tire through which the contestant must jump.

Toilet area: A designated spot in the yard where a dog goes to defecate and urinate.

Track age: Time lapse between tracklaying and tracking attempt.

Track faithful/track sure: Tracking dog's quality to concentrate solely on the track.

Track happy: Fun-loving dog that makes a game of tracking without commitment.

Track scent: Combined ground scents of disturbed vegetation and animal odors.

Tracking harness: Padded, non-restrictive harness worn by tracking dog.

Tracking line: 40-foot line attached to tracking harness used to handle tracking dog in competition.

Tracklayer: Person responsible for establishing track in competitive event.

Trailing: Following airborne scent.

Trainability: Dog's ability and desire to learn; propensity of a dog to focus on handler and accept direction.

Training ring: Ring on training collar to which leash is snapped.

Umbilical hernia: Congenital outpouching of abdominal tissues resulting from lack of fusion of muscles.

Undershot: Lower incisors protruding beyond uppers.

Wait: Command used to tell dog that you will return shortly.

Weave poles: Agility obstacle consisting of sticks protruding from ground, through which dog must weave.

Weight pulling: Competition in which dogs match strength and ability to move weighted sled or wagon.

Window jump: Agility obstacle consisting of suspended window frame through which competitor must jump.

Wooden dumbbell: Article used in scent determination part of Obedience trials.

Work-play balance: Essential part of any training that refers to the necessity to intermingle training with play.

Worm check: Fecal examination to determine endoparasite infestation.

Yard ball: Hollow, firm plastic ball that is too large for dog to pick up, yet small enough to be tossed about by using top of muzzle and feet.

Index